PRACTISING COMMUNITY DEVELOPMENT

Community Development Foundation

The Community Development Foundation (CDF) (formerly known as Community Projects Foundation) was set up in 1968 to pioneer new forms of community development.

CDF's role is to show how to involve people in the regeneration of their communities, through a broad programme which includes consultancies, training, local action projects, publications, conferences and research. CDF aims to demonstrate the most effective ways to:

- help people participate in community action and public affairs;
- increase the sensitivity of public authorities to local needs and hopes;
- develop working partnerships between public and private agencies and community groups;
- bring about public policies that regenerate community life.

Chairman: Alan Haselhurst
Chief Executive: David N. Thomas

Community Development Foundation
60 Highbury Grove London N5 2AG
Tel: (071) 226 5375

Practising Community Development

Experience in Strathclyde

Alan Barr

COMMUNITY DEVELOPMENT FOUNDATION
•PUBLICATIONS•

First published 1991 by
the Community Development Foundation
60 Highbury Grove
London N5 2AG
Registered Charity Number 306130

Typeset by Stanford Desktop Publishing Services, Milton Keynes
Cover design by Peter Taylor of the Production House
Printed in Great Britain by Elmtree Graphics Ltd, Colchester

British Library Cataloguing in Publication Data is available
from the British Library

ISBN 0 902406 63 9

Contents

Foreword

No public authority in Britain has invested in community work on as large a scale as the Strathclyde Regional Council. They are a Labour Council who are aware of the weaknesses of conventional democratic procedures as a means of representing people – and particularly the most deprived and excluded people. They see community work as a way of giving themselves firmer roots among those whom they were elected to serve, and giving the people a stronger voice in shaping the development and priorities of public services.

Having established this pioneering, and sometimes controversial work, the Council's Social Work Department had the courage to invite Alan Barr – an experienced community worker teaching at the University of Glasgow – to make an independent study of the community work services based in the Department. (There are community workers in other Departments too.) Then, critical though some of Dr Barr's findings were, they were happy to see them published in this book so that their experience could be shared with others interested in this field.

Thus far, most of the research on community work has dealt with the more glamorous initiatives such as the community development projects set up by the Home Office. It tends to be full of drama and conflict, but short on conclusions which might help those concerned with the long haul. Here, however, is a study of the daily work of an established service which has moved beyond experiment and rhetoric – a study, too, which relates its findings to the whole literature on communities and community work. It should be widely read.

Alan Barr, the Strathclyde Regional Council and the Community Development Foundation which publishes this book deserve the thanks of everyone interested in this field.

Alan presents his own findings throughout the book and distils their essential principles in his final pages. I shall not offer yet another summary here. But as someone who has been associated with his research over the years I may be able to pose a few questions which will start readers thinking and help them to make fuller use of the pages which follow.

The Strathclyde Regional Council has adopted carefully considered priorities on which it has built a 'social strategy' that is designed to help the poorest people and the poorest neighbourhoods. This provides guidelines and a framework for community development, along with all the Region's services. The strategy, most regional councillors would admit, does not work as well as it should; and it certainly does not eliminate all the conflicts between community workers and the state. Nevertheless, it provides a statement of fundamental aims and values to which all concerned can refer when trying to resolve dilemmas and conflicts.

This leads to my first set of questions. Can community work operate effectively without a clear commitment to basic principles and priorities of this kind? If I am right in believing it cannot, then public authorities which do not accept Strathclyde's 'bias to the Poor' (to use a phrase familiar in the churches) must ask themselves what other priorities their staff are to follow in their work and to convey to the public. Without guiding principles or a corporate personality of any kind, workers who venture out from behind the protective screens and counters of the public services to engage more openly with the people will either go to pieces, or confine themselves to safe but trivial routines (booking halls and taking the minutes of meetings), or become guerillas sniping at their employers on behalf of their most noisily aggrieved customers.

Underlying the methods of community work, there are principles which are both scientific and moral. Their scientific basis lies in the recurring observation that we do not fully understand human problems, and cannot therefore formulate fully effective responses to them if we do not give the people who experience them a voice both in the analysis of the problems and in the formulation of solutions. Other voices must be heard too. But a study of the needs of the unemployed (or of one-parent families or people with AIDS, or whoever...) which does not give a voice to those people will – to some degree at least – get it wrong.

A good case could be made for consulting people on moral grounds of courtesy or humanity, or just on grounds of political expediency. But consultation promised for these reasons rarely confers real power on the poorest people when hard decisions have to be made about scarce resources. That's why they are poor: powerful people can afford to neglect them.

The scientific argument that to give the victims a voice in the discussion is an essential requirement for arriving at the truth, may help us to think more honestly about the power relations involved, and the various ways in which people can be given a voice that will not be disregarded.

Community work is one way of giving people a voice. But it is not, as a profession, the only instrument available for this purpose. Community workers did not invent the community-based way of working, and they are – fortunately – not the only profession to use it.

Frank Kitson (then a Brigadier, but later General Sir Frank) was laying down similar principles for soldiers in his book *Low Intensity Operations* nearly 20 years ago. Lord Scarman, after the Brixton riots, gave the same advice to the police: crime prevention has to be a community-based, hearts-and-minds operation or it is worthless. The medical profession – another with strongly authoritarian traditions – is increasingly adopting the same principles. You cannot stop people smoking by giving people pills or lectures.

This leads to my next set of questions. As more and more professions adopt, for their own good reasons, community-based ways of working, what should be the special contributions of community workers? How can they be trained and deployed to help in carrying these methods of working forward everywhere, without relieving ordinary policemen, doctors and others of their obligations to listen to the people and work with them? We do not want a band of specialists whose existence encourages other professions to say, 'we leave all that to our community worker'.

If they are sound, the principles of community work apply to every profession that works with people. They are not just for other people to take note of: we have to ask how they would apply to whatever we are doing. Which may not be a comfortable thought.

This thought has special significance for those of us who work as applied social scientists in tertiary education. It is not too difficult to see how the people who experience the problems that we study can be given a voice in our research – even though it is too seldom effectively done. But how do we give them a voice in our teaching? How many of those who train probation officers and prison officers ensure that their students listen with respect to offenders telling of their own experiences? How many give the offenders a voice in planning the training itself? (Those who have good answers to these questions should perhaps be asked to turn their attention next to barristers and judges.) How do we give mental patients a voice in the education of doctors and psychiatric nurses...council tenants a voice in the training of housing managers?

And how do we set up courses in these matters which the customers of the services concerned could themselves take? It takes years to train a housing manager, but we encourage council tenants to set up housing co-operatives with little, if any, education. How do we teach – and learn from – the people who are (in Barbara Wootton's immortal phrase) 'more planned against than planning'?

Professor David Donnison
University of Glasgow

Editorial Preface

Community development is now increasingly accepted as a central strategy for local authorities intent on fostering collaborative and accountable relationships with their citizens. In England, the publication of the AMA Report, *Community Development: the Local Authority Role* in 1989 symbolised this acceptance.

In Scotland, Strathclyde Regional Council adopted community development as a central element of its anti-deprivation strategy from its inception in 1975. This commitment, by the largest local authority in Western Europe, and sustained over 15 years, contains important lessons for community workers, local authorities and public policy-makers.

This important book draws on two field investigations of community work practice. The first, undertaken in 1983, required community workers across Strathclyde to keep accurate records of their use of time on a minute-by-minute basis over a month. These workers were subsequently interviewed about their practice priorities. The second investigation was undertaken in 1989 and was not as rigorous but involved an audit of community work in the Social Work Department based on interviews with community work teams and a questionnaire to all staff.

Strathclyde Region has a strong commitment to community development. This is expressed in a number of ways, particularly in the underlying principles of its social strategy and previous policy documents, and in its employment of community workers or community-related officials in a number of departments. In particular, the Education Department, which provides a community education service across the Region, is notable for its contribution to community development.

However, this study focuses on the experience of community development within the Social Work Department. It is the workers here who have been at the forefront of the Council's anti-deprivation strategy, located as they are in the designated areas of priority treatment.

The book is in four parts. The first provides an historical overview of community development in Strathclyde and the final section explores the lessons to be learnt from this experience. Parts II and III examine the detailed evidence from the two field studies from which the conclusions in the final part are drawn.

The Community Development Foundation is privileged to publish this book in the knowledge that it makes an important contribution to community development at a critical time. We look to the 1990s as a decade when it will come of age, with a sound practice base and a recognised role.

This book deserves wide readership, not only among community workers and local authorities but also amongst those concerned with the decentralisation of local government, community-based service delivery strategies and the empowerment of citizens.

Stuart Hashagen
Manager, Scotland
Community Development Foundation

Acknowledgements

My thanks for their assistance in relation to the 1983 research are due to several people: Fiona Lees, Fiona Thomas and Naomi Graham who were seconded from the Strathclyde Regional Council Social Work Department to work on data collection; Bill Longdon (also seconded from the Social Work Department) and Mary Brailey for their assistance in the time budget analysis; Frances Dick, Lottie Wallace and Margo McCafferty for secretarial services; Philip Bryers and Bryce Anderson of Strathclyde Regional Social Work Department; Professor David Donnison for much valued supervision and advice. I would also like to record my gratitude for the support of Professor Fred Martin, my former head of department, whose untimely death terminated his involvement in the study, and for the assistance of his successor, Professor Rex Taylor.

Equally, I would like to thank the community work staff who were the subjects of the enquiry who co-operated with such good will and the Social Work Department and its Director, Professor Fred Edwards, for its openness in supporting the study and providing ready access to its staff.

Finally, I would like to thank the Community Development Foundation and particularly its Scotland Manager, Stuart Hashagen, for his support and assistance, as well as Charlie McConnell, Gabriel Chanan and Catriona May. My thanks also to Linda Brawley at the CDF Scotland office for secretarial services.

Part I
The Study and its Context

1

Community Development in Strathclyde

Introduction

A comparison between Strathclyde and the UK as a whole indicates the relatively late emergence of community development north of the border and a much greater emphasis on employment in local authority departments. It may be argued that the social, political and economic conditions surrounding the emergence of community development in Strathclyde from the mid-1970s were markedly different from those prevailing almost a decade earlier when community work in other parts of the UK took off. The 1960s was the period of the so-called 'rediscovery of poverty'. Macmillan's 'never had it so good' era was being demonstrated by Townsend, Abel-Smith[1] and others not to be a universal experience. Poverty was perceived, however, against a backcloth of growing prosperity. A belief in continued economic growth and affluence based on a technologically-advanced productive base seemed to hold within it the potential for eradication of poverty as a phenomenon. The late 1960s too, particularly for the educated young, was a period in which there was a sense of optimism about the potential for political and social change, illustrated most forcibly in the eruption of radical direct action politics of protest. Movements like Students for a Democratic Society in the United States, the anti-Vietnam war protests, the Civil Rights movement, the French alliance between students and workers culminating in the near revolution of May 1968, the Czechoslovakian liberalisation movement and similar events around the world were reflected in the youth politics of Britain. Many workers entering community work in the late 1960s had themselves been political activists, and were drawn to it as an expression of their personal ideologies. They seemed to believe in the potential for radical social change through the mobilisation of disadvantaged people in their communities. What is more, the language of some of the official documents of programmes like the Community Development Project[2] seemed to contain similar hopes, though these were often contradictory.

Community work in this period emerged as an expression of radical aspiration when there was optimism and energy for change. However, the realities of practice soon led workers to question the sophistication of their analysis of the problems.[3] With increasing understanding of the intractability of the structural roots of many problems, optimism gave way to a sense of disillusion for some and realism for many. 'Large hopes' contrasted with 'small realities'.[4]

By the time community work took off into significant growth in Strathclyde the era of romantic optimism in community work was almost over. However, it can be argued that it was not only that understanding had changed but that in many senses the West of Scotland had never been the cradle of the post-war affluent society. As the statistics from the 1971 census indicated, the conurbation had a record of social disadvantage unparalleled in mainland Britain. Poverty was pervasive, and as such it was probably more difficult to romanticise about the potential for its elimination. Community work as part of an anti-deprivation strategy emerged without expression of the grandiose expectations which accompanied it in the late 1960s. Indeed, Regional Council policy statements specifically acknowledged the degree to which many problems were outside the scope of local influence and stressed the need for realism.

These differences of historical context are highly significant and should be borne in mind when exploring the evidence of this research, not only in terms of what the workers actually spend their time doing but also in terms of the aspirations that they hold for their work.

The dominance of employment of community workers in local authority departments in Strathclyde is a further distinction from other parts of the UK. This, too, may be a reflection of the period of its development in that not having experimented with community work during its early, highly volatile period, the local authority avoided some of the destructive conflicts experienced elsewhere. It was able to learn from these and develop a more considered approach. Whilst there are still inconsistencies within its policy, Strathclyde has arguably one of the most developed and explicit policy frameworks for community work practice formulated in the light of almost a decade of developments elsewhere, as well as experience in some of the former authorities drawn into the Region by local government restructuring.

There are other possible explanations for the dominance of statutory sector employment of community workers in the Region. It may derive from the view of key politicians and officers of the Regional Council that, if it were to respond to the problems of deprivation, it should do so in co-operation with the community itself. To do this it was necessary to generate internal mechanisms in disadvantaged areas which would enable them to give expression to their concerns and enter into participation with the Council. Community work was the means to achieve this. However, this does not explain why Strathclyde Regional Council should choose to adopt this approach when other Scottish Regional Authorities and their equivalents in the English Metropolitan County Councils generally did not.

It may be argued that the Scottish Regions, having more extensive powers, particularly in the areas of education and social work, have the organisational means to develop community work and to develop integrated social policy for their areas. But this does not explain why Strathclyde is the exception amongst Scottish Regional Councils. In this respect the explanation may lie partly in the concentration of the problems of urban Scotland within its boundaries and partly in its sheer scale. Perhaps more significantly, the virtually unassailable position of the Labour party in controlling the Regional Council has made it possible to develop a long-term planned approach to change, in the expectation of continuing in power. In my view though, the critical factors may well be to do with time-specific conditions which created the potential for innovation.

The emergence of key individuals, both members and officers, who were positively disposed to the use of community work methods in a newly-formed and potentially powerful authority, with a Labour government in power, ideologically committed to respond to the relatively disadvantaged position of the Region, and themselves untainted by a defensiveness about earlier failure to effectively address these conditions, were probably the key factors.

With these broad themes in mind, the more detailed history of development can be explored.

Early History of Community Work in the Region

Statutory Initiatives

Prior to the Scottish local government reorganisation in 1975, two of the local authorities later to be drawn into the Regional Council had been hosts to central government projects. In the Ferguslie Park area of Paisley was located the only Scottish project of the 12 in the Home Office CDP Programme, whilst the Craigneuk area of Motherwell was the setting for the only Scottish Comprehensive Community Project. Though the Ferguslie Community Development Project played its part in the national developments, it tended to be rather geographically isolated and concentrated on neighbourhood development work and action research, particularly focused around public sector housing issues of lettings, maintenance and repairs, employment and advice and information services. The Craigneuk project, despite the grand title, was also focused on neighbourhood work rather than the corporate local planning orientation of its English counterparts. In that both of these projects provided a local focus for the debates developing more extensively south of the border, they were significant in contributing to the preconditions which influenced Regional policy development.

The local authorities themselves, prior to reorganisation, had not generally become involved in community work but there were some notable and significant exceptions. In the education departments of the pre-reorganisation authorities, the *Alexander Report*[5] recorded 45 community centre warden posts in 1972 but these appear to have largely focused on the management of centre-based service provision. In Ayrshire, however, almost in anticipation of the direction to be taken by the *Alexander Report*, there had been the emergence of outreach work from community centres to local neighbourhoods, thus placing workers from this setting in a much more developmental than service-providing role. Indeed the thrust of provision in Ayrshire had taken on such a general orientation to community development that prior to 1975 it was known as Community Development Services.

It is worth noting that the Regional Council Policy Review Group on community development services which reported two years after reorganisation said: 'community education, reflecting community development principles, has had only limited impact to date on the education department itself though there are notable exceptions in particular areas and particular schools.[6]

The developments in the education sector were acknowledged then as limited and there was an implicit indication in the statement that not all community education work could be equated with community development.

More significant in relation to the focus of this study on the social work sector, there had been neighbourhood community development initiatives established in the Gibshill and Strone and Maukinhill areas of Greenock. The former, initiated in 1969[7] adopted a generally non-directive stance towards the development of the community which began to develop and run services for itself, particularly in the area of youth provision, though also campaigning effectively on the issue of housing improvement. The latter, starting a few years later, was to reflect a growing national trend towards corporate management and formalised structures of community participation in the development of community planning. The project involved the employment of a community planner in the Planning Department alongside a community worker in the Social Work Department. In evaluating this project[8] the workers were sceptical about the effectiveness of the consultative procedures adopted to involve local people in the planning of their areas but were more positive about the direct campaigning activities of community groups over local issues. In that later Regional policy was to include similar local corporate management and participation procedures, this is a significant conclusion.

Significant too is the fact that prime movers behind the Greenock projects, the Social Work Director, and his Chairman, were to continue to be highly influential in the development of community work in the post-reorganisation period. The latter was also Director of the Local Government Unit at Paisley College which acted as a highly significant 'think tank' for community development in the region during this period, both generating and disseminating relevant literature.

Voluntary Activities

In the period prior to reorganisation, the voluntary sector had also produced significant initiatives, though mainly in Glasgow. The chief exceptions to this were the Community Projects Foundation work in Barrowfield, and the Strone and Maukinhill Informal Education Project in Greenock[9] which was sponsored by the Rowntree Trust. The latter focused on the promotion of locally-based adult education initiatives responding to locally-expressed needs. The Social Work Committee Chairman was again influential in the promotion of this project.

It was in Glasgow, however, that the most influential voluntary sector initiative had developed. This was the Crossroads Youth and Community Association in Gorbals and later Govanhill.[10] It grew out of the worker priest movement, a group ministry having been founded in the area in the late 1950s, oriented to social action. They launched the first community newspaper in Scotland and became involved in a variety of housing campaigns, play projects, youth provision and other activities. From an emphasis on advocacy roles on the behalf of the community, the group became more involved in the promotion of community-run initiatives. When formally established in 1967, the Crossroads organisation was created to manage two youth workers and still consisted largely of outsiders to the area. It later promoted two student units for the training of community workers, and it was pressure from the staff of the units which led to Crossroads management being taken over by local people. From a service tradition, not dissimilar to the settlement movement, therefore, emerged a community-managed organisation which, in the period just before and after local government reorganisation, became involved in a highly conflictual community action campaign against damp housing in the newly developed Gorbals.

The early animateur of much of this development was the Rev. Geoff Shaw who, as a Labour councillor and the first Convenor of Strathclyde Regional Council, was to be a very significant influence in the early policy developments on deprivation and community work.

The community action tradition with which Crossroads has come to be associated (though it in fact continues also to be extensively involved in service-oriented activity) was not extensive in Glasgow but the Gairbraid tenants campaign[11] over redevelopment is also worthy of note.

Local Government Reorganisation

Social Conditions in Strathclyde

By the time of local government reorganisation in 1975 there were, thus, a few dispersed developments which were to be influential in the emergence of an anti-deprivation strategy, not least because key figures in these initiatives moved into powerful political and administrative positions in the new structure. The conditions for innovation were enhanced by the creation of a new authority, of scale, with a sense of its own power and unfettered by defensiveness about historical failures to address problems of deprivation.

The reorganisation of local government in Scotland, following the *Local Government Scotland Act* 1973, was based on a structure of Regional and District Councils, and led to the creation of Strathclyde as the largest local authority in Scotland. The Region, which has a population of 2.5 million people, includes nearly half the Scottish population. Though the Region encompasses a wide hinterland of the highlands and islands to the north and west and the lowlands to the south, its population is concentrated around Glasgow and the industrial towns of the Clyde valley like Greenock and Dumbarton in the west, Hamilton and Motherwell to the south. Though Glasgow exhibited the worst features, all of these Clyde corridor towns were shown in the 1971 census to be suffering from a high degree of multiple deprivation relative to other parts of the UK. Holterman[12] in an analysis of the 1971 census data demonstrated that, in terms of deprivation, Strathclyde was in a league of its own.

Taking the enumeration districts with conditions which locate them in the worst 5% in the UK, the number of such districts in Strathclyde as a percentage of the enumeration districts in the conurbation on five key indicators was as shown in Table 1.1 (see p. 10).

Table 1.1 Comparison of Strathclyde with next worst conurbation in relation to percentage of enumeration districts falling into the worst 5% for the U.K. on five indicators of deprivation (Source : Holterman, 1975)

Variable	Strathclyde	Next Worst Conurbation
Overcrowding (+ 1.5 persons per room)	44%	14% (inner London)
Household share or lack hot water	18%	17% (inner London)
Household without exclusive use of all amenities	16%	13% (inner London)
Household with no car	30%	18% (Tyneside)
Economically active males unemployed but seeking work	27%	18% (Merseyside)

Comparing Strathclyde with Scotland as a whole, the Region contained 90% of the enumeration districts in the worst 1%, 80% of those in the worst 2% to 5% and 79% of those in the worst 6% to 10%.

One-quarter of all children lived in overcrowded houses and the infant mortality rate was twice the national average. Evidence from the National Child Development Study reinforced this picture in its report *Born to Fail*.[13] Though the statistics were not published until 1982, the second report of the study *Children in Adversity*[14] relating to 16-year-olds in 1974 said:

'Our earlier study highlighted the problems of Scotland particularly the Glasgow area, and our new findings confirm the situation. Ten per cent of Scottish children were disadvantaged at 11 or 16, twice the proportion in England and Wales.'

A Social Strategy
The Labour-controlled Council which took office in Strathclyde in 1975 was committed to make a response to these conditions and evolved a social strategy to combat deprivation. A feature

of this strategy was to be community development. From a few pockets of community work activity, prior to reorganisation, grew a major commitment to community work. The initial council statement on multiple deprivation[15] focused on three responses to the problem: increased corporate working; community development and regeneration; and the identification of areas of priority treatment for positive discrimination in the deployment of council resources.

This strategy was based on an eclectic view of the causal explanations of poverty and deprivation. The report talked of three factors:

> 'First, the main issues, which are nationwide and arise out of the socio-economic situation which has emerged in the West of Scotland since the 1950's... Secondly, the difficulties arising from the attitudes, nature and scale of provision of public services – health education, police, social work, transport, leisure and recreation, housing, cleansing, job centres and social benefits... Thirdly, the problems associated with the communities themselves.'

How adequate the responses proposed could be to the way the problems were defined, was obviously an open question, for whilst structural and institutional arguments were being recognised, the Council acknowledged that its services tended to presume pathological explanations. However, it began by identifying 45 areas to be given priority in terms of local authority services and a further report, *Areas of Need – the Next Step*[16] was prepared, particularly exploring the approach to be taken in the seven areas selected as Special Initiative areas. In these areas there was to be special attention to local corporate working supported through the appointment of area initiative co-ordinators employed by the Chief Executive's Department.

A Community Development Policy

Also following the multiple deprivation report, the Council set up a policy review group on community development which, in commenting on earlier multiple deprivation strategy reports, stated:[17]

> 'Those documents identified the need for a coordinated effort by our departments and by regions and districts, a failure by

our departments to deal in terms of people rather than tasks, poor information services, a sense of estrangement from councillors and M.P's; the need for stimulation of self help activities and local leadership; and the need for authorities to allow communities a genuine voice in the running of their areas.'

The same report, which came to be known as the *Worthington Report*, went on to suggest that 'every Regional employee must come to see himself as a community development worker'[18] but its concentration was on the development of community work in the Social Work and Education Departments of the Authority. In identifying its perception of the community work task the Report stated:[19]

'community work is essentially two pronged – the worker should not only be concerned with meeting the needs of the groups with which he works in the community, but also with working within his own department so as to improve its internal knowledge of community problems and aspirations in the hope of ultimately modifying its policies and practices in ways which are to the communities advantage.'

The report stressed the need for realism about the outcomes of community work. Criticising what were seen as the grandiose ambitions of the national Community Development Project and other earlier programmes it comments: 'there was then a feeling that community work could solve the problems of deprived areas. This is about as realistic as expecting a flea to push an elephant uphill'.[20]

The Policy Review Group on Community Development Services set the basic framework within which the Regional Council has promoted community work activity for the last decade. The group decided not to establish a separate community development department but to sustain a significant community development presence in both the Social Work and Education Departments. However, it did propose the establishment of a Community Development Committee to 'secure coordination of community development services throughout the Region' and 'manage Community Education and Social Work Community Development including responsibility for resource allocation'.[21] A full committee of the Council therefore took responsibility for a particular part of the activities of two of its service departments which remained responsible to their own committees.

The policy review group also proposed the establishment of area development teams. These were to be local corporate management and community participation structures not dissimilar to those that had been employed by the Strone and Maukinhill Community Planning project. They would consist of: 'a core group of workers from the Departments of Education, Social Work (and where possible) Strathclyde Police' and 'would be chaired by the local Regional member'. They would 'seek the active cooperation of District members/officers and Community Councils'.[22]

Their functions included identifying community needs and 'co-ordinated' solutions, liaison with community councils and voluntary organisations, study and comment on the deployment of community work staff and resources and monitoring of the impact of Council policies.

This proposal and the subsequent development of the teams illustrates a tension in the Regional policy between a corporate management/community planning approach operating through participation procedures limited to the statutory Community Councils, and a more radical approach based on the provision of support to local community groups working on their own issues in their own terms. This is a continuing theme of this study. The tension is well illustrated by comparison of the underlying ideology of the policy review group report of 1978 and the 1984 consultative Report of the Director of Social Work, *Helping the Community to Organise*.[23]

Community Development in the Social Work Department

Helping the Community to Organise clarified the philosophical basis and objectives for community work in The Social Work Department. An extensive commitment to community work is justified by reference to the statutory obligation of social work authorities under the *Social Work (Scotland) Act* 1968 to 'promote Social Welfare' and further supported by reference to Scottish Office circulars following that Act. In particular, the Report quotes Circular (SW11/69) which notes that the promotion of social welfare involves 'the development of conditions whether for individuals, for families or for larger groups, which will

enable them to deal with difficulties as they arise through their
own resources or with the help of the resources of their own
community'.[24]

Helping the Community to Organise states: 'The basic distinguishing feature of community work is that its primary focus
within the process of community development is on assisting
communities to organise around locally defined needs and
issues.' It goes on later to state: 'community work involves a
form of 'dialogue' between residents and workers who are also
accountable to their employing agency for the content of their
activities.'[25]

Throughout the development of community work in the
Region there has been a dual emphasis on the promotion of
autonomous local community organisations and on working
within the departments of the Regional Council to better inform
and influence their policies and service delivery. Workers in this
position are accountable to the Department and expected to
reflect its policies, whilst simultaneously influencing their evo-
lution and change. This is a situation ripe for experience of role
confusion, and the evidence of the research study emphasises
some of these problems.

Tensions in Regional Community Development Policy

Comparison of the policy review group Report and the later
consultative document reveals differences in orientation to community work within the Regional Council but so too do the performance criteria for community work suggested by the former,
when compared with the explanations of deprivation favoured
in the Council's *Multiple Deprivation* report of 1976. The review
group suggested 'reduced crime, reduced vandalism, reduction
in the rate of emigration from an area, better services through
pressure, staffing stability, more clubs and societies and high
membership, provision of community facilities'.[26]

Such criteria suggest more pathological explanations of the
problem than the more structural explanations favoured in the
original policy document.

Claims that the Regional Council has an entirely coherent and
consistent policy for community work should therefore be questioned.[27]

In view of the focus of this book on community work practice in the Social Work Department, it is worth dwelling more extensively on the practice philosophy indicated by the Director's consultative report. Further to the quotations above he goes on to say:[28]

'Its emphasis is on promoting forms of local social organisation which are self determining and relatively autonomous. Within the terms of the Council's social strategy, this involves assisting disadvantaged communities to mobilise their interests, skills and resources around current needs or issues in such a way as to achieve desired or realistic change.

There are a number of intended outcomes of community organisations of this kind. Effective local community organisations will define and express local needs in ways which require a response from local authority services and from within the community's own resources. This should result in improved local services both by and for the community. It will also involve increased community access to resources and to the processes of decision-making regarding local resource allocation.'

Later he states:

'Whatever the position, *The community worker's role is never that of representing or speaking on behalf of the community, nor is it to be the advocate of Council policies to the community*. The worker's primary concern is to assist the community to maintain a dialogue with the authority at a level and in a form appropriate to the issue in question. In this sense the community worker is not a "mediator" bringing sides together, but more of a "consultant" and an enabler to the community' [author's emphasis].[29]

The objectives of practice identified in the Director's consultative document, though suggesting some inconsistency with earlier statements of intent in the community development policy review report, are however consistent with the most significant Regional Council policy statement on the deprivation strategy. The report *Social Strategy for the Eighties* (1985) recognises some of the confused expectations surrounding community development by the Regional Council. It identifies progress in the establishment of the Community Development Committee, the appointment of an increased number of community workers, a £2m a year budget for community projects, the establishment of 20 area development teams, the organisation of six community conferences and the setting up of a decentralised system of small grants committees. But it goes on to say:[30]

> 'The "community approach" has become a fashionable phrase which conceals more than it reveals. There seems to be a consensus about the desirability of something called community development/involvement/participation. But behind that consensus lies confusion. At one extreme it may reflect a deliberate or unconscious attempt to ensure a more orderly acceptance of policies and services: at another it might express a genuine desire to shift the balance of political power. In between there is a lot of confusion – and no little paternalism with assumptions that it is communities, or groups within communities, who need changing or developing. It is our view that it was rather the policies and procedures of public agencies that needed changing or developing. In espousing community development we needed the active support of residents. Support here does not mean harmonious consensus. Many people in local government seem to think that clients of statutory services should have a subservient and grateful relationship to local government and that collective organisation and protest is impertinent and unseemly.
>
> What they seem to want from community involvement is public approval if not applause! By "support" we mean strong collective organisation to press from below – whether by example or by argument – for the sorts of improvements we indicated in 1976 we wished to see from our nominal positions of power. Because what many of us have recognised is the illusion of being able to use such power and authority to engage on our own in significant change.'

This extract indicates the climate of debate about community work surrounding the workers who became the subject of the research. Some of the confusions in the character of their work and their perceptions of them reflect debates within their employing authority. Workers no doubt both contributed to the debate and were caught up in the tensions between paternalistic and empowerment models of practice. By 1985 the Regional Council was clearly recognising empowerment models, and this is a considerable shift from some of the assumptions made about the purposes of community development in the early stages of the policy development when the *Worthington Report*[31] identified 'four persistent threads' in the idea of community development. First: 'The creation of a sense of belonging to an area and the strengthening of community networks ...' Second: 'the encouragement and stimulation of self-help activities ...' Third: 'The identification and stimulation of local leadership ...' Fourth: 'The need for an effective respectful and sympathetic response by the authorities in making resources available and in providing services appropriate to the area's needs ...' Though the last of these goes on to refer to 'devolving power' and 'increasing community influence on decisions,' the general tenor of the theoretical orientation reflects a conservative model of practice and contrasts markedly with references to 'collective organisation and protest' in the *Social Strategy for the Eighties* extract above.

These tensions have continued to be present as community development policy has evolved in the latter half of the decade. The *Social Strategy for the Eighties* continues to provide the policy framework. It emphasises work in the specified Areas of Priority Treatment with particular attention to five major themes – poverty, housing, health, employment and community development – and six key policy areas – adult education, pre-fives, elderly, youth services, unemployed people and single parents. Alongside this policy has emerged a parallel economic strategy the terms of which are set out in a policy statement entitled *Generating Change*.[32] This policy recognises that economic regeneration is fundamental to responding to deprivation and poverty. Emphasis continues to be given to positive discrimination towards disadvantaged neighbourhoods but greater attention is given to promotion of community-based economic enterprise and public/private sector investment in partnerships. Amongst a range of responses, the Region has extensively supported the community business movement through Strathclyde Community Business, encouraged local employment in priority areas, created a £5m venture capital fund from its Superannuation Fund, and invested in training programmes. Perhaps most significantly, it has established its own Social and Economic Initiatives in peripheral estates like Easterhouse and Drumchapel, entered into joint working with central government in New Life for Urban Scotland Partnerships in Castlemilk

and Ferguslie Park, and is working in partnership with District
Councils in schemes such as the East End Management
Structure which succeeded the Glasgow East End Renewal
Project (GEAR).

These and other economic initiatives promoted within the
Region have had significant implications for community
workers. In their Foreword to *Generating Change* the leader of
the Council and the Chief Executive summarise the basis of the
economic strategy. They state:[33]

> 'With high unemployment and tight financial restraints on
> local authority spending, the council has encouraged the
> development of successful partnerships with private compa-
> nies as well as with other agencies and with the people in the
> communities...
>
> We believe that pioneering work has won important
> rewards for the communities and for employment.
> Developments of this kind will be encouraged with enthusi-
> asm.'

It is apparent from this summary that though a community orientation is sustained, the economic strategy seeks partnerships
with private capital institutions and therefore has to come to
terms with the motivations which underpin private investment.
These may have more to do with 'healthy' returns on capital
than relieving deprivation. Though the policy continues to talk
of 'empowering local people', there is clearly an increased
tension between locally-generated development and externally-
negotiated schemes introduced into areas for their benefit but
with limited community involvement. Such a tension may be
inevitable, but where community workers are operating in initiative and partnership areas, they are experiencing considerable
pressure to engage local communities in the process of deliver-
ing objectives which have not evolved locally. The tension
between social planning (and in some areas, for example,
through deliberate attention to diversifying housing markets,
social engineering) and community development focused on
'assisting communities to organise around locally-defined needs
and issues'[34] is readily apparent. Nonetheless it is difficult to
conceive of an effective anti-deprivation strategy which does not
deliver economic opportunity. In the 'enterprise culture' of the

late 1980s perhaps such tensions are to be anticipated as the back cloth to community work.

Associated with the emergence of the Generating Change Strategy has been an increased involvement of the Chief Executive's Department in community development. Its primary roles are in sustaining a corporate overview of community development strategy through servicing of divisional community development committees and area liaison committees. Generating change has extended its role in employment of co-ordinating staff in Initiative Areas and led to the creation of a training unit. The department also has a small unemployment unit. The primarily economic regeneration orientation of Chief Executive's department staff contrasts with the primarily social regeneration orientation of staff in the Social Work Department.

Two other significant changes in the second half of the decade should also be noted. First, the regional community development committee was replaced by five divisional community development committees which report to the social strategy sub-committee of the policy and resources committee. These in turn have replaced corporate divisional deprivational groups. The second significant change has been in relation to corporate structures in the areas for priority treatment (APTs). The 20 area development teams have been replaced by area liaison committees (ALCs). The former were local government officer and elected member groups, whereas the latter involve local community participation. ALCs now operate in most APTs. Local variations, often influenced by the perspective of the local elected member, have resulted in very different patterns of community participation evolving in different areas.

Taking account of the range of developments in the Region, the policy context for the practice of the workers studied is complex. It does, however, appear to provide scope for community work activity across a wide variety of approaches.

Concluding Comment

As a footnote to this discussion, it is worth speculating as to why the Region has made such a commitment to community development.

Hall et al[35] have argued that three main criteria determine the significance that an issue achieves in policy terms. First, its legitimacy, in which they ask: 'is this an issue with which government considers it should be concerned?' Secondly, its feasibility, in which they identify three major factors, 'the structure and distribution of theoretical and technical knowledge'; 'particular ideologies, interests, prejudices and information' and 'concern about resources, collaboration and administrative capacity'. Thirdly, the level of support is identified as crucial, although whose support is significant varies under different conditions. In other words, it is not simply a matter of electoral support but may equally relate to party political support or professional/administrative support.

Adopting these three criteria, it can be argued that the publication of the analysis of the 1971 census results legitimised deprivation as a central policy concern for the Regional Council, for the disadvantages of the region were subjects of national debate and concern. The legitimacy of a community work approach to this problem is less easily understood, for by 1975 the conflicts surrounding the activity, particularly as a result of the Community Development Projects, were well known. However, in relation to these conflicts, key people in Strathclyde were publicly identified with the arguments of the project staff rather than their sponsors. Indeed, the early policy documents on the deprivation strategy, even if sceptical about the degree of change which could result, drew directly from analysis generated in the Community Development Project programme. In terms of feasibility it has been noted that in formulating their policies, the Strathclyde planners were able to draw on the acquired knowledge and technical skills tested in earlier community work projects. There also existed among key people an ideological commitment to community work as an approach and the Urban Programme provided a potential resource base from which the plans could be implemented. In terms of support the electoral base may not have been critical, for it was an explicit commitment of the Labour party to tackle deprivation, and the power base was felt to be secure. The internal support of the Labour members was probably more significant. Officer support existed in key positions though one of the continuing problems of the Authority has been to generate a general level of officer commitment to the purposes and processes of the deprivation strategy.

Combined, these factors appear to have prompted the inno-
vations which the research explored. By 1983 (the date of the
original research) the Social Work Department employed 120
community workers and by 1989 the number had risen to 189.
This is approximately 90% of community work staff in all
Scottish Social Work Departments. For comparison, the
Community Education Department employs approximately
twice this number but their responsibilities are divided between
adult education and youth work as well as community work.
The emergence of community development staff in the Chief
Executive's Department has previously been noted.

Notes

1. B. Abel-Smith and P. Townsend, *The Poor and the Poorest*
(London: Bell, 1965).
2. For a discussion of the CDP programme see M. Loney,
Community Against Government (London: Heineman, 1983).
3. See for example J. Benington, 'The flaw in the pluralist heaven:
changing strategies in the Coventry C.D.P' in R. Lees and G.
Smith, *Action – Research in Community Development* (London:
Routledge and Kegan Paul, 1975).
4. H. Specht 'The Dilemmas of Community Work in the United
Kingdom', *Policy and Politics*, vol 4, no. 1 (1975).
5. K.J.W. Alexander, *Adult Education: the Challenge of Change* ('the
Alexander Report') (Edinburgh: HMSO, 1975).
6. A. Worthington, *Policy Review Group on Community Development
Services* ('the Worthington Report') (Strathclyde Regional
Council, 1978) p. 6.
7. S. Mackay and L. Herman, *A View from the Hill* (Paisley: Local
Government Research Unit, Paisley College of Technology,
1980).
8. S. Hashagan, 'Making and Breaking the Rules', *Strathclyde
Studies in Community Work*, Occasional Papers, vol II (1982).
9. C. McConnell, 'Community Education in Scotland' in L. Smith
and D. Jones, *Deprivation, Participation and Community Action*
(London: Routledge and Kegan Paul, 1981).
10. B. Bryant and R. Bryant, *Change and Conflict – a Study of
Community Work in Glasgow* (Aberdeen University Press, 1982).
11. S. Jacobs, *The Right to a Decent House* (London: Routledge and
Kegan Paul, 1976).
12. S. Holterman, *Census Indicators of Urban Deprivation*, Working
Note 6 (London: Department of the Environment, 1975).
13. P. Wedge and H. Prosser, *Born to Fail* (London: National
Children's Bureau and Arrow, 1973).

14.   P. Wedge and J. Essen, *Children in Adversity* (London: National Children's Bureau and Pan, 1982) p. 30.
15.   Strathclyde Regional Council, *Multiple Deprivation* (1976) p. 6.
16.   Strathclyde Regional Council, *Areas of Need – the Next Step* (1976).
17.   *The Worthington Report*, p. 11.
18.   Ibid. p. 19.
19.   Ibid. p. 28.
20.   Ibid. p. 45.
21.   Ibid. pp. 14, 48.
22.   Ibid. pp. 14, 50.
23.   Director of Social Work, *Helping the Community to Organise*, (Strathclyde Regional Council, 1984) para. 1.3.
24.   Ibid. para. 3.4.
25.   Ibid. para. 3.10
26.   *The Worthington Report*, p. 46.
27.   For a fuller discussion of the early Strathclyde policy, see C. McConnell, *Deprivation and Community Development Policy in Strathclyde – an Analysis and a Critique* (Dundee College of Education, 1978).
28.   Director of Social Work, *Helping the Community*, para. 43.4.
29.   Ibid. para. 4.5.
30.   Strathclyde Regional Council, *Social Strategy for the Eighties* (1985) p. 26.
31.   *The Worthington Report*, pp. 4–5.
32.   Strathclyde Regional Council, *Generating Change: Urban Regeneration: The Strathclyde Experience: Opportunities for Private Investment* (1987).
33.   Ibid. p. 3.
34.   Director of Social Work, *Helping the Community*, para. 3.4
35.   P. Hall, H. Land, R. Parker, A. Webb, *Change, Choice and Conflict in Social Policy* (London: Heinemann, 1975) pp. 475–486.

2

About the Study

The Relevance of the Study

'Much of the British community work literature which is currently influential came out of the ad hoc projects of the late 1960s and early 1970s... One unfortunate consequence of this feature of our home grown literature is the inadequate attention paid to the development of long term programmes in established agencies such as social service departments.'[1]

Baldock's comment reflects one of the motivating factors behind the research on which this book is based. Among social work departments in the UK, Strathclyde is not only the largest but also one which has invested more than most in community work. A study of the community work undertaken within it is therefore a study of long-term work in an established agency.

Though the material for this book is derived from study of community work within a social work department, it is important to recognise that both the characteristics of the practitioners and their work are not peculiarly relevant to social work settings. The issues raised have extensive implications for community development in any local authority context.

Since Strathclyde Social Work Department employs a large number of community work staff, the study is an exploration of a substantial investment in community work as a strategy for social change. Whilst there are still issues regarding its relationship to established social work functions and practitioners, community work in the department has not been marginal to other activities.

Community development in Strathclyde is part of a corporate anti-deprivation policy. The contribution of community workers, whether in Social Work, Education or other departments, was seen as responding to the concerns expressed by local communities rather than the particular interests of the host department. Equally it was seen as having corporate implications.

In the early days of the strategy, community work units, though managed by the Social Work Department, generally functioned relatively independently of other areas of social work practice. More recently, integration into the Department has been seen as important, though community workers are not expected primarily to service conventional social work client group needs. A report[2] reviewing community work in the Region in 1989 identifies three main roles for community work:

'a) enabling local people to define, articulate and resolve issues of concern to them,
  b) researching and producing recommendations about policy issues affecting community development in the broadest sense,
  c) promoting the creation of local social services for traditional social work clientele through community work activity, for example, self help initiatives.'

It is important to note that the substantial majority of the community workers employed within the Social Work Department are not trained as social workers but have youth and community work or other relevant qualifications. In this respect they have a distinct identity which is shared with most community work staff employed in the Education and other departments.

Taking all these factors into account it will be evident that lessons from this study have applicability to any local authority context from which community development practice is promoted.

The Focus of the Study

Strathclyde has an explicit and well-developed policy framework for community development and itself claims to have moved beyond hopeful rhetoric.[3] Despite this it should not be assumed that the character of the work which has developed in the field is fully understood either by the sponsors or practitioners. This is not surprising. Employment of professional workers in any area of activity results in an interaction between the collective and individual dispositions of the workers and the intent of policy. By their very nature, policies designed to respond to complex and ill-understood problems like multiple deprivation will tend to lack consistency. As a result they are open to different interpretations which will reflect the motivations of those employed to implement them. The displacement of the intended goals of policy may equally significantly be affected by the attitudes of consumers. This is particularly true in community work where the outcome of any initiative is largely, if not wholly, dependent on the reaction of local people. A worker has to recognise the substantial influence of the goals of the community itself if it is to be seen as a central resource in the resolution of its own problems. This constitutes a major and largely uncontrollable variable in the community work process which, alongside employing agency intent and workers dispositions, results in complex interaction, negotiation and 'trade-off' which produce the actual character of community work activity.

The dynamic relationship between the sponsors and their policies, the workers themselves, the managers of the service agency in which they are based and the consumers of their activity provides a core focus of this study. The research examines this relationship primarily from the perspective of the community work staff but also seeks an objective view of the work which is actually undertaken.

From its own perspective, each party to the relationship may have a different understanding of the nature and functions of community work. Myths and confusions abound. It is vital to know, therefore, what the practitioners actually do and to appreciate their motivation and perceptions of their role. Failure to clarify the nature of the activity is to court the sustaining of unrealistic expectations. When these are unfulfilled by the outcomes of practice,anger and frustration is the result.

Material to explore these issues was collected first in a substantial research project in 1983 and has been supplemented for this publication by a follow up audit of the state of community work in the Social Work Department in 1989.

The Aims of the Research

The aims of the original research were straightforward. They were to move beyond the statements of intent to examine how community workers actually spent their time, what motivated them and how they viewed the other parties to the community work process – the elected members, their managers and the consumer groups. The research proposal stated:

'In itself a description of how community workers are spending their time and a statement of the purposes which they perceive this activity to have would be of fundamental importance. If resources are to continue to be expended on community work activity it is essential that accurate descriptive investigation is undertaken to provide a basis for more rational and realistic policy formulation.'

Variations in patterns of work revealed by the study would assist in examining with workers why they operated as they did. The evidence would also provide material to consider the influence of different theoretical models of community work practice.

The descriptive material focused on three distinct elements of practice. First, the characteristics of the community work practitioners. Secondly, the ways in which they spent their work time and their relationships with other people involved in community work. Thirdly, the value dispositions of workers towards their own practice and their employers.

Three distinct methods were used for data collection. To establish basic information about worker characteristics, each worker was interviewed employing a closed question questionnaire. To identify the character of work and the networks of contact involved, workers, with advice and support from research assistants, maintained detailed, hour-by-hour diary records of their activities for a four-week period. A set of categories of activity and their contents was derived from these recordings. To explore their attitudes and values, the workers were interviewed, following their diary recordings, using an interview schedule largely employing open-ended questions.

The audit of the state of community work practice undertaken in the autumn of 1989 has facilitated comparison with the earlier findings. The audit firstly involved a questionnaire to all community work staff identifying current areas of work, the objectives of these, the degree of collaboration with other agencies, and specifying the factors currently affecting community work practice which workers believed required attention.

Secondly, meetings were held with each of the 30 community work teams to discuss practice issues.

Characteristics of the Workers Studied

The 1983 research examined all four categories of community work staff employed by the Social Work Department at that time. The most senior, the Community Development Organisers, carried both field management and local social planning functions. They were accountable to the managers of the Social Work Districts. Below them, in a line management role, were the Senior Community Workers who were directly responsible for supervision of staff. The most substantial group of these were the basic grade, qualified, Community Workers. The others were Community Work Assistants who were unqualified staff largely recruited from the ranks of community activists. There has been a continuing debate as to whether their role is to assist community work staff or to work independently as unqualified community workers.

The pattern of community work employment parallels the relationship between Area Officers, Senior Social Workers, Social Workers and Social Work Assistants in social work practice.

The research sample represented 50% of each category of staff. It consisted of six Community Development Organisers, five Senior Community Workers, twenty-seven Community Workers and eighteen Community Work Assistants.

Overall men outnumbered women 3:2. There was an inverse relationship between gender and seniority in that women were not represented at all in the most senior group of workers but outnumbered men in the most junior.

The age distribution of the sample was remarkable in its lack of correlation with seniority and its indication of the youthfulness of the workers. The mean average age was 32.1 years; for Community Development Organisers 33.5; Senior Community Workers 33.6; Community Workers 30.8; and Community Work Assistants 33.1.

If we were to attempt to construct a portrait of the typical worker in each of the categories in the 1983 research, the Community Development Organiser would be male in his early thirties and the holder of a social science degree and a professional qualification in youth and community work. He would have been likely to have worked for a short period in an occupation unrelated to community work, to have had at least one other community work post but for less than two years prior to entering his present post, which he would have occupied for about four years. He would have had little or no voluntary work experience.

The typical Senior Community Worker would also be male in his early thirties. He would be professionally qualified in youth and community work or social work but would not hold a degree. He would have had at least one previous community work post and have occupied it for substantially longer than the Community Development Organiser. He would have held his current post for about two years. He would be likely to have been employed in a related occupation for more than three years before entering community work. He would have had limited involvement in voluntary work for about three years.

The typical Community Worker would again be male and about thirty years of age. He would be unlikely to hold a degree, though he would be professionally qualified most probably in youth and community work. He would be less likely than the previous two categories to have worked in a non-related occupation but would probably have worked for a couple of years in a related occupation, most probably in an unqualified capacity in social work. He would have held one previous community work post but for a period of less than two years and would have also occupied his present post for less than two years. His voluntary work experience would be both more extensive and substantial than for the previous two groups of workers.

The typical Community Work Assistant, by contrast with the other groups of workers, would be female, though again in her early thirties. She would have three or four 'O' levels and possibly one higher. She would have no higher education and hence no professional qualification. She would have worked for more than four years in an occupation unrelated to community work but have had an extensive and substantial degree of voluntary work most probably relating to children in her own neighbourhood. She would not have held a community work post before and would have occupied her present post for less than two years.

By 1989 there had been some notable changes in the organisation of community work. A reorganisation of the Social Work Department in 1986 led to the integration of community work teams into the line management structure of area social work teams. The Community Development Organiser post disappeared, these workers being redeployed most commonly as Assistants to the managers of the twelve districts into which the department was divided or as Area Managers of social work teams. An increased number of Senior Community Workers were appointed but the other levels of Community Worker and Community Work Assistants remained as before though continuing to grow in numbers.

In terms of personal characteristics there has been little change except that many community workers have been longer in post and the average ages have risen.

Notes

1. P. Baldock, 'Community Work and the Social Services Departments' in G. Craig, N. Derricourt and M. Loney, *Community Work and the State* (London: Routledge and Kegan Paul, 1982) p. 24.
2. Strathclyde Region Social Work Department, 'Review of Community Work' (unpublished, 1989) p. 4.
3. Strathclyde Regional Council, *Social Strategy for the Eighties* (1985).

Part II
The Nature of Community Work

3

What Do Community Workers Do?

There appears to be much public confusion about what community workers actually do. Indeed community workers may themselves be as prone to fantasy about the nature of their occupation as external observers. Particularly in relation to campaigning work involving direct forms of political action, there is a tendency to glamorise the nature of the work. Clearly, away from the publicity, much of the work is mundane and routine. Yet it is most probably the quality of the unglamorous and less visible roles which is as crucial in community work as in other activities.

Fantasy also seems to be reflected in the way in which workers frequently present the types of work with which they are involved. This may be a reflection of the difference between aspiration and actuality, associated with a desire to present a radical self-image.

In the light of the potentially distorted public perceptions of community work it is important to clarify what workers actually do. The 1983 time-budget research and the audit of practice in 1989 provide different but compatible insights into the nature of practice. The former addressed a number of questions. How much time for example do community workers spend working directly with other people? How much time is spent in formal meetings of community organisations or professional groups compared with the time spent working in informal ways with individuals? To which problem areas is most time given: housing, unemployment, women's issues, children and young people, provision of community premises and amenities, the elderly or others? Do workers operate in a planned or reactive manner? Is their work focused on campaigning activities or directed towards the development of local services in the community? Does seniority increase the degree to which work focuses on the needs of the employing organisation relative to the needs of the community which it serves?

It is important in examining the evidence from the 1983 time budget study to recognise that it provides a picture of what a group of community workers was doing in a given month rather than an impression of the tasks involved in the overall execution of a community work intervention.

The 1989 audit was simpler in approach, requiring all workers to indicate the range of community groups with which they were working. Whereas the 1983 diary recordings allowed measurement of relative commitment of time to different activities, this material only provides a measure of numbers of community groups focused on different needs at a particular point in time. However, it does provide a detailed breakdown of the community needs to which workers address themselves with community groups. It also provides a basis for comparing the work patterns of the different categories of worker, namely Community Work Assistants, Community Workers and Senior Community Workers.

The 1983 Time Budget Study Findings

The analysis of the 1983 data on a time-budget basis (that is, how much time is given to different activities) produced a mass of detail of how workers spent their time. This section concentrates on the major trends which illustrate the roles which community workers undertake and by implication the skills which this may involve. Reference will be made in commenting on the findings to the Regional Council document *Helping the Community to Organise*[1] which sets out the expectations of the Social Work Department of the role that community work staff should undertake.

It is useful first to distinguish between two sorts of activity, non-contact activities, which occupied 22.4% of worker time overall, and contact activities, occupying 77.6% of time. The former are activities which do not involve the workers in any direct form of contact with other people whilst the latter are ones in which they are engaged directly with other people. As with other aspects of the time budget it is not possible to compare these findings with other studies. Judgement of whether such a distribution of time should be regarded as normal is therefore subjective. The activities were examined not only in terms of the typical amounts of time allocated to them but also in terms of the numbers of workers who engaged in the different activities. This latter measure provides a better basis for assessing whether workers undertake the kinds of activity which the literature suggests that they would be likely to. It is important to remember, however, that though not engaged in some activities during the recorded month, their overall practice may well still involve them in these activities.

Non-contact Activities
In terms of total time allocated to non-contact activities there was not a wide variation between the four groups in the 1983 sample, though it is perhaps interesting that the Community Development Organisers spent least time in this activity.

The most substantial and extensive activity was writing, accounting for 6.6% of workers' time. The content analysis shows that this was most commonly recording and report writing, but that written work relating to administrative tasks was almost as common. Writing in relation to information gathering and research work was also of note, and for Community Workers, writing for community newspapers and preparation of grant applications were significant features.

Though not quite universal, reading and information collection was the second most substantial activity though only taking up half as much time as writing. This appears quite often to have involved joint work with colleagues. Again, the activity often appears related to administrative tasks. Work related to housing campaigns figures significantly for Community Workers and Community Work Assistants.

If the percentages of time allocated to writing and reading are translated into actual time, a typical worker would have spent approximately two-and-a-half hours writing and one hour and twenty minutes in reading and information collection per week. Given the significance attached in the practice theory literature of community work to recording, monitoring and evaluation of work and the demands on workers to keep abreast of developments in their area of work, this does not appear to be a very substantial amount of time. A CCETSW study[2] suggests that the worker 'requires the ability to stand back and appraise the situation and evaluate the strengths and weaknesses of, for example, those with whom he is going to work and the feasibility of achieving the goals which a community group may be setting itself'.

Given that this activity heading also includes the preparation of reports and applications for funds for projects, and that it will later be shown that helping to obtain resources was the most extensive form of work undertaken, the time given to systematic reflective information gathering and writing is even more limited. Generally it is held that it is the early stages in community work intervention, of identifying community needs and resources, that involve workers in most information gathering and associated writing. Even after this stage it is assumed that these activities must continue in order to see how the situation may be changing and whether the workers' intervention may be regarded as influential. Given the short length of time that many workers had been in post (see Chapter 2) it would be reasonable to anticipate that many workers would still be involved in the preliminary stage of getting to know the community. However, this evidence is discouraging for those who believe that this should involve extensive investigation.

Travel was the next most substantial non-contact activity, followed by the almost universal activity of administration. At 3.4% of worker time it was not a major activity, though it should be noted that some of this work scored under other headings.

Administration of resources accounted for just 1.4% of time overall and relates primarily to the provision of community premises, facilities and amenities.

Time spent planning workload was not very significant, scoring less than 1% of time overall and only being recorded by 50% of the sample. This finding will be discouraging to those who believe community work to require a systematic planned approach to change and may, in part at least, explain the high level of contact time which appeared to be unplanned.

Overall, the analysis of non-contact activities does not reveal a substantial level of attention to reflection or analysis of work undertaken. Whilst this may be regarded as generally problematic for community work, it is likely to be particularly so in relation to Community Development Organisers whom the Director of Social Work[3] argued should 'consolidate their role as social planners'.

Contact Activities

Turning to the contact activities, Table 3.1 (see p. 39), giving the percentages of time allocated to each activity and Table 3.2 (see p. 40), the number of workers recording activity in each category, provide the basis for a general assessment.

The activity category occupying most time overall was 'other non-planned contacts' though its significance was almost matched by the category 'other pre-planned contacts'. The categories both refer to contacts with others which were not part of a programme of arranged meetings. The difference between them is that the former happened by chance whilst the latter was pre-arranged with agreement as to the purpose of the contact. Both occupied around 16% of time for the sample as a whole, but there were clear variations between the groups in the sample which demonstrated that more senior workers, especially Community Development Organisers, were less involved in unplanned contacts whilst more junior workers, especially Community Work Assistants, were more extensively involved in them.

It may be argued that the managerial role of Community Development Organisers and Seniors gave scope for a greater degree of control over the process of work, whereas the field-work focus of the other two groups of workers placed them in an inherently more unstructured working environment. In other words, managerial roles are more amenable to a pro-active approach based on the authority of the worker relative to those with whom contact is made, whereas fieldwork is likely to be more reactive to events which may precipitate the worker into unanticipated contacts. Less charitably though, it could be argued that the extensiveness of unplanned contact time might have been a reflection of uncertainty and lack of direction in the worker's activity which indicates lack of systematic forethought about the purposes of intervention in the community. The latter suggestion is supported by the evidence of how non-contact time was used.

The third most common activity was 'meetings of non-statutory organisations for non-social purposes', which accounted for 12% of time overall. Again, this was a universal activity. The category was a composite one containing meetings both of community organisations and professional groupings. The network of contacts involved and the analysis of the content of these meetings shows that Community Development Organisers were predominantly involved in inter-professional groupings and Community Workers and Community Work Assistants with meetings of community groups.

This would be anticipated from the roles defined by the Social Work Director[4] for each group of workers. Community Development Organisers were expected to take on 'social planning' roles and to have 'oversight of local community work' rather than be directly involved in practice. Seniors, though 'retaining an element of community work practice' had staff supervision as their 'primary role' supplemented by 'liaison with social work teams and with other agencies locally'. The practice of community work was seen as the province of Community Workers and Community Work Assistants.

Table 3.1 provides the time allocations for the remaining categories and their rank order for the sample as a whole and each group. There appears to be a broad distinction to be drawn between the work activities of Community Work Assistants and Community Workers compared with the two more senior groups in the sample. Thus the former scored more highly in relation to doing things with others non-social, regular social groups (mainly Community Work Assistants), being available (that is, at specified times to be contacted), home visits, being supervised, and public meetings. The latter scored more highly in relation to telephone calls, (marginally) correspondence, supervising, interviewing. The pattern of time allocation between activities is reflected in the findings of the network analysis, discussed in the next Chapter, which generally showed much more extensive and substantial contacts of a professional nature for Community Development Organisers and Senior Community Workers, and more extensive and substantial community contacts for the other two groups. This is consistent with the role definition of each group of workers.

Some of the findings of the activity analysis are most interesting for their lack of significance in the time budgeting of the workers. Public meetings, meetings of Community Councils, meetings of Regional or District Council Committees, and community surveys all scored low.

A simple mean average for time spent in a particular activity may not reveal uneven distribution across the sample. Table 3.2 shows the number of workers recording time spent in each activity. This illustrates, for example that only 29% of the sample were involved in Community Council meetings during the recorded month. Similarly, it shows that 41% of Community

Work Assistants, 46% of Community Workers and 80% of Seniors received no supervision during the recorded month.

Table 3.1 Contact activities as a percentage of overall time allocation by worker group in overall rank order

Category	CWA	Rank	CW	Rank	SCW	Rank	CDO	Rank	All
Other non-planned contacts	18.7	1	17.1	1	13.2	2	10.1	3	16.5
Other pre-planned contacts	12.6	2	16.5	2	17.2	1	22.9	1	16.2
Meetings of non-statutory organisations (non-social)	10.4	3	13.5	3	13.2	3	11.4	2	12.3
Phone calls:									
incoming	1.6)		1.1)		1.7)		2.9)		2.4)
outgoing	2.7)	7	3.5)	5	4.6)	5	2.4)	5	3.3)
unspecified	0.1)		0.4)		0.1)		0.5)		0.3)
Conferences and courses	5.4	5	5.1	4	2.0	10	4.7	7	4.9
Doing things with others non-social	5.6	4	4.0	6	3.9	8	1.6	9	4.2
Team/staff meetings	3.2	8	3.6	7	2.1	9	3.0	8	3.3
Correspondence:									
incoming	0.1)		0.7)		3.1)		2.9)		1.2)
outgoing	0.4)	12	1.9)	8	1.1)	7	1.8)	6	1.4)
unspecified	0)		0.4)		0)		0.4)		0.3)
Regular groups – social	4.8	6	0.8	17	-	-	0.2	16	2.0
Supervising	0.1	19	0.5	18	6.8	4	7.4	4	1.8
Being available at specified times	1.8	9	1.3	9	0.3	13	-	-	1.3
Home visits	1.7	10	1.0	13	0.1	15	0.7	12	1.2
Union meetings	0.2	18	1.1	11	5.5	6	0.4	13	1.1
Being supervised	1.6	11	0.9	14	0.3	13	-	-	1.0
One-off organised events	0.9	14	1.1	10	-	-	0.4	13	0.9
Interviewing for staff	-	-	0.9	14	1.4	11	1.5	10	0.7
Community Council meetings	0.4	15	0.9	14	1.0	12	0.1	15	0.7
Public meetings	0.3	16	1.1	12	-	-	-	-	0.7
Committee meetings of Regional or District Council	1.0	13	0.2	20	-	-	0.8	11	0.5
Community surveys	0.3	17	0.2	19	-	-	-	-	0.2

Table 3.2 Number of workers by group engaging in contact activities

Category	CWA	CW	Senior	CDO	Total
Other pre-planned contacts	17	26	5	6	54
Other non-planned contacts	17	26	5	6	54
Meetings of non-statutory organisations (non-social)	17	26	5	6	54
Phone Calls:					
incoming	17	23	5	6	52
outgoing	17	26	5	6	54
unspecified	1	13	2	3	26
Conferences and courses	9	12	2	3	26
Doing things with others (non-social)	17	22	5	4	4
Team/staff meetings	13	21	3	4	41
Correspondence: incoming	14	21	5	6	46
outgoing	13	25	5	6	49
unspecified	1	6	1	1	9
Regular groups social	11	6	-	2	19
Supervising	1	4	4	5	14
Being available at specified times	4	7	1	-	12
Home visits	12	17	1	1	31
Union meetings	6	10	3	1	20
Being supervised	14	10	1	-	25
One-off organised events	7	9	-	3	19
Interviewing for staff	-	4	1	3	19
Interviewing for staff	-	4	1	3	8
Community Council meetings	4	9	2	1	16
Public meetings	4	11	-	-	15
Committee meetings of Regional or District Council	1	2	-	3	6
Community surveys	4	3	-	-	7

This table also suggests that there may have been anomalous patterns of work within particular worker groups arising from the idiosyncrasies of particular workers. One Community Development Organiser, for example, accounted for all home visits by that group and one Senior for a substantial proportion of the union involvement.

Examining the broad pattern of time allocation between contact activities, Community Workers and Community Work

Assistants can be seen to have held similar activity patterns, as can Community Development Organisers and Senior Community Workers. However, a more detailed examination of the contents of these activities and the networks of contact involved (see Chapter 4) reveals some significant variations, as well as similarities in the pattern.

Content of Activities

Whilst it is interesting to consider the kinds of activities which the workers undertake, the character of their practice is much more illuminatingly revealed through examination of the content of these activities. Provision of community premises, facilities and amenities was the most commonly occurring category of content in the recordings. For the overall sample it was ranked in the top five categories of content in 12 separate activities. This category of content was an important element of Community Workers' recordings in the following activities – meetings with non-statutory organisations and regular groups (non-social), other pre-planned contacts, other non-planned contacts, telephone calls, correspondence. It also featured prominently in Community Council meetings, public meetings, being supervised, supervising, management of resources and planning workload, but as there were small proportions of time devoted to these activities their content is of lesser significance. In the major time-consuming activities, the content category of provision of community premises, facilities and amenities, has a similar prominence for all sub-groups of workers studied.

The content category resource work also featured prominently in the content analysis overall, showing up in the first five content categories for ten separate activities, including the large, time-consuming activities mentioned above. These activities involve work to obtain the financial means to promote community activities and services, for example preparing applications to local grants committees. Here, however, Community Workers recorded this element of work content markedly more than Community Work Assistants. It can be concluded that Community Workers made a greater contribution than Community Work Assistants to providing advice about supporting or assessing community groups' resource needs. At the time of the recordings, the resources in question were largely associated with summer play schemes and their financing. The management and administrative responsibilities of the more senior workers probably accounted for the relative prominence of the category resource work in several activity headings. For Community Development Organisers, resource work features substantially in 11 separate activity headings. In the activity headings, meetings of non-statutory organisations and regular groups (non-social) and correspondence, the content of work for Community Development Organisers was first and foremost the assessment of and provision of financial and material assistance for community development activities. For Senior Community Workers this was also important, but to a lesser extent.

The content analysis revealed that two categories of content provision of community premises, facilities and amenities and resource work were of major importance for community work staff at field level. As the responses to the final interviews indicated, these elements of community workers' duties were believed by the workers to be highly valued by community organisations and expected by employing authorities. However, they are not aspects that appear to receive much attention in discussions among community workers or in the literature. It may be argued that such routine servicing of community organisations and groups is a necessary stage before development of wider community group activity can take place; such categories of content of community work are potentially instrumental to the achievement of other change activities.That these roles should have such prominence is perhaps surprising in the light of the images that community workers often project about themselves but it is entirely consistent with the expectations placed on workers by their sponsoring department.

Regional Council Expectations of Community Workers

It is interesting to compare the expectations of community work roles with the evidence both in the 1983 study and the 1989 study. In his 1984 review of community work, the Director of Social Work[5] identified ten areas of community work activity. These were information, advice and resource services; housing and the environment; children and parents; elderly and handicapped groups; claimants; the unemployed; health issues, women's issues; legal services and the use of legislation; race relations.

Information, advice and resource services corresponds very closely in its description to the activities identified above under the headings of provision of community premises facilities and amenities, and resource work. He assesses these as the primary functions of community work and says:[6]

'The basic approach of community workers has been to provide to groups the information, advice and other services and resources they require to operate effectively as local organisations. Any group which is mobilised around a particular issue or need requires relevant information, a local base, and access to typing and reprographic facilities.'

The 1983 findings show that this was the primary role of workers at that time. By 1989, though housing and environmental issues had become the most frequent concern, advice information and resourcing remained central. Workers were extensively engaged in support to community organisations providing infra-structured supports to community development – meeting places, typing and reprographic facilities, information and advice services, production of community newspapers. Even within the housing category, much of the work also involved provision of information to groups particularly in relation to the *Housing (Scotland) Act* 1988 and the implications of 'tenant choice'.

The second form of activity listed by the Director of Social Work is housing and the environment. He suggested[7] this had been a predominant and sometimes 'contentious' area of work. Whilst the campaigning style of work on housing does appear to feed the images of community work commonly being involved in conflict, the evidence of the 1983 analysis of the recordings did not indicate this activity to be as widespread as might have been anticipated. Work in this area was recorded under two headings: predictably, work with housing campaigns, but also work with tenants associations. The latter did not exclusively concern housing but this was heavily predominant. Neither category scored highly, suggesting both that housing was not as central an issue as assumed and that more conflicting community action styles may have had more visibility than extensiveness.

However, by 1989 housing and environmental issues had become the most frequent focus of activity. From a total listing of 934 community organisations with which workers worked,

19% were directly concerned with housing and environmental issues and a further 9% were multi-functional groups for whom these issues were a component of their concerns. This compares with 16% of groups whose primary function was resourcing or information and advice provision.

The growth of attention to housing appears largely attributable to the impact of the *Housing (Scotland) Act* 1988. From the time of the White Paper preceding this legislation, its radical implications, particularly in diversifying housing markets and altering tenancy arrangements, precipitated widespread concern among public sector housing tenants. As Strathclyde Region has the highest proportion of public sector housing in the UK, the level of attention by community workers to housing issues is readily explicable.

The third area of community work activity identified by the Director of Social Work was children and parents. This corresponds with the 1983 content category intermediate treatment/youth and children's work. The writer suspects that the Director did not refer to the youth work dimension directly as there is often contention between the Community Education and Social Work departments as to whether the latter has a role in this area. The evidence of the research is that workers believe they do. The Director states:[8]

'The majority of APT's have high proportions of children whose families are likely to be on low incomes and lack necessary material and social support. The proportion of single parents in these areas is also likely to be high. The individual and social needs associated with poverty are compounded by poor local facilities and services and high transport costs. There is a clear role for Community Workers, in association with other social work and education staff, to promote forms of local organisations which seek to secure necessary services for children and their parents.'

For Community Workers and Community Work Assistants, the content category intermediate treatment/youth and children's work was significant in several activities, though it achieved top ranking in only one activity, regular groups (social). This aspect of work was to some degree magnified by the seasonal duties connected with the planning for and preparation of Easter and summer holiday play schemes. However, it was clear that

Community Work Assistants had a greater role in contact work with youth and children.

The 1989 audit, however, shows a very similar level of worker contact with groups concerned with children, between Community Work Assistants and Community Workers though the former appear to have more contact with youth groups and less with single parents. Overall, by 1989 the ranking of children, youth and parent work was the third most frequent form of activity representing 15% of groups worked with. A high proportion of this work (30% approximately) related to support to play schemes. Other substantial children's activities were support to link up groups of professional workers and parents concerned with children's needs and creche provision. In relation to youth work it was noticeable that workers were more involved in strategic planning of youth provision and youth action groups than in direct youth service provision which falls to the Community Education Service.

The next major theme of work identified by the Director of Social Work was elderly and handicapped groups.[9] In the 1983 study these were subsumed under the heading of community care and community service schemes, indicating the character of work undertaken with the two groups. This was an important area of activity but mainly for Community Work Assistants. By 1989 it was not appropriate to categorise work with elderly or handicapped people under the community care or service label, for the predominant focus of activity had moved to support for campaigning organisations of elderly and disabled people. This transformation reflects an important change in attitude amongst community workers as well as the groups themselves and also suggests a welcome politicisation of issues of ageing and disablement.

Though Community Work Assistants were still more likely to be involved in these areas of work than their qualified colleagues, the general level of attention had increased. In all, 6.5% of the groups worked with focused on needs of elderly people, and 3% disabled people.

At the time of the 1983 study it was noted that in some respects the content analysis results were as interesting in terms of what they did not show. For example, there was very limited attention to work focused on women's issues; whilst health concerns may have been a sub-theme of other areas of work, health rarely emerged as a primary focus; race was not central nor were legal services or work with unemployed people. Between 1983 and 1989 there appears to have been a substantial diversification of community work practice and some of these categories of work are now more prominent. It was noticeable, however, in the 1989 audit that when each team of community workers was invited to identify major themes of their work they tended to over-estimate the degree of change, suggesting that aspirations for practice and realities may not match. Work on health and women's issues had grown but still represented only 4% and 3% respectively of groups worked with. It is fair to point out that both health and women's issues were a component part of other activities, for example housing and environment in relation to the former and children and parents in relation to the latter.

Work with claimants and unemployed people has also increased but this work is now subsumed under a general category of local economy work. The 1989 audit suggests three broad divisions to this work: firstly, attention to income maximisation and support schemes, most notably food cooperatives, but also credit unions; secondly, promotion of community businesses and local employment projects; and thirdly, investigation of the characteristics and working of the local economy to inform wider campaigns and social and economic planning processes. Overall, 7.5% of groups worked with relate to local economy issues and amongst these income support and maximisation projects predominate.

In his 1984 report the Director of Social Work[10] noted the specialist nature of legal services and this remains an undeveloped area of practice. Race also remains a marginal issue. Due to the geographical concentration of ethnic minority groups it is not altogether surprising that anti-racist and multi-cultural work is infrequently reported. Nonetheless, given increased evidence and awareness of racist attitudes and behaviours in the West of Scotland, more attention would be justified.

In both the 1983 and 1989 studies attention was given to the level of corporate working by community work staff. In the earlier study this form of work, defined as collaborative work with staff of one or more other department of the Regional or District Council, was not extensive except for Community Development Organisers. For them this activity scored heavily in the categories of meetings of non-statutory organisations, regular groups (non-social), team meetings and other pre-planned contacts. At that time Senior Community Workers were involved to a lesser degree but by 1989, partly since they had taken on many of the duties of Community Development Organisers (that post having ceased to exist), the involvement was extensive. It primarily related to the emergence of Area Liaison Committees for which many Senior Community Workers act as lead officers. Corporate working has also become more significant for the other categories of worker but to a lesser extent.

Perhaps a surprising outcome of the 1983 content analysis was that work with a forum/network of community groups was found to be a prominent category of content in only the small (in terms of time spent) activity headings – public meetings and management of resources. This probably reflected a generally parochial neighbourhood orientation on the part of workers as revealed in their responses to the final interviews (see Chapter 8). By 1989 the number of federal groups had increased somewhat and workers were collaborating across neighbourhoods to a higher degree, particularly on housing matters, though such contacts were still not extensive.

Notes

1. Director of Social Work, *Helping the Community to Organise,* (Strathclyde Regional Council, 1984).
2. Central Council for Education and Training in Social Work, *Social Work Curriculum Study – the Teaching of Community Work* (1974) p. 4.
3. Director of Social Work, *Helping the Community,* para. 9.3.
4. Ibid. paras 9.1, 9.6.
5. Ibid. para. 5.2.
6. Ibid.
7. Ibid. para. 5.8.
8. Ibid. para. 5.13.
9. Ibid. para. 5.20.
10. Ibid. para. 5.41.

4

Who Do Community Workers Work With?

In examining the work which community workers undertake, some of the broad trends relating to whom workers have most contact will have become apparent. The purpose of this Chapter is to provide a more detailed exploration of the nature and patterns of the contacts between workers and other parties. The interest of the material lies in the answers it offers to a number of questions. At a basic level, does community work involve more time being spent with members of the community, other professional workers or politicians? Within each of these groups, what are the most significant sub-divisions? For example, is it the case that community workers meet large numbers of members of the community in the process of their work or are their contacts largely restricted to the small numbers of people who are the active members of community groups? Does the fact that the workers are employed in the Social Work Department mean that their inter-professional contacts are mainly with other departmental employees or do they cross boundaries into other departments or the non-statutory sector? Within their own departmental colleagues is it primarily other community workers with whom they spend time or is there a significant interface with social workers? Is there extensive contact with managerial staff of their own department? To what degree are these contacts with others created purposefully and to what extent are they simply a product of people being in the same place at the same time? To what degree are there variations in the patterns of contact for different designations of worker, for example do Community Development Organisers spend more time with managerial staff and politicians, or Community Workers and Community Work Assistants more time with community groups? What are the predominant contents of contacts with the different groups?

The answers to these questions are interesting in themselves in so far as they help to demystify the nature of community work. They also help to clarify its organisational character and the nature of the knowledge and skills required of community workers.

Material in this chapter is primarily drawn from the 1983 study with some comparison with the 1989 audit. In the initial questionnaire to workers, data was collected about both their personal characteristics and the organisational features of their work. This provides a useful entry to a discussion of who workers work with.

Organisational Context

Examining the locations from which the workers operated, the most notable feature from the 1983 study was the complicated variety of work bases. 27% operated from area social work teams and 30% from community development teams at a district level. Most of the latter were located in district social work headquarters. 16% operated from Special Projects or Area Initiatives and 20% from community flats or their equivalent. All the Community Development Organisers were located in district headquarters but their degree of contact with their staff varied enormously depending where the latter were located. 37% of workers (entirely made up of Community Workers and Community Work Assistants) also operated from another base, most usually a community flat. Only 11% of workers were not located with at least one other community work colleague, Community Development Organisers being more likely to be isolated than their colleagues. Overall, 50% of workers operated alongside three or less colleagues and 50% more than three. Community Work Assistants were more likely to be part of smaller groups.

The complex pattern of work locations no doubt contributed to the equally complex lines of accountability as understood by the workers. Community Development Organisers all saw themselves as accountable to district managers, Seniors generally worked to Community Development Organisers, though one related primarily to an Area Officer. Community Workers most commonly saw themselves as accountable to the Community Development Organiser or Senior Community Worker, but Area Officers, Project Leaders and District Managers also figured. Interestingly, only one Community Work Assistant saw himself as primarily accountable to the Community Development Organiser alone, accountability to Senior Community Workers or Community Workers being more common.

Information on location of workers suggested that 78% could have been expected to be in contact with other social work staff as a result of the location of their work place. Few were in settings where they were located with other professional agencies related to community work.

By 1989, despite the intervening restructuring of community work, remarkably little had changed in relation to organisational functions. The Community Development Organiser post had gone and workers were now much clearer about their accountability through the Senior Community Workers and then the area social work Manager. However, despite being linked into the area social work team structure, workers were not necessarily located with those teams though generally speaking the Seniors to whom they are accountable were. 80% of Seniors were in area teams but 52% of Community Work Assistants and 45% of Community Workers still operated from other premises; most notably local community flats on housing estates. Although Seniors were usually located in area team premises, 38% of them had responsibility for workers located in more than one area social work team. Physical proximity of workers to their managers remains an issue for although few workers operate in isolation, many are quite detached from their senior colleagues. It is still the case that most workers are in premises where other social work staff also operate, but it is not common for them to be located alongside other professional agencies. In non-area team premises there are usually high levels of day-to-day contact with members of local communities.

Comment on Organisational Location

The evidence relating to the location and accountability of workers provides some valuable insights into the organisational nature of community work. It is immediately apparent that the practice of the workers is characterised by what Smith[1] has called its 'front line' nature. Though community work is bureaucratically organised with line management accountability ultimately running through to the Director of Social Work, the physical location of most workers is distant from a central management hierarchy. Indeed, many workers operate either totally, or for a significant part of their time, away from immediate contact with their line managers to whom they are accountable. As will be shown later, in discussion of the factors which influence the way in which workers practice, they claimed a quite high degree of autonomy in interpreting their roles in the community. This may partly be related to their physical location which is an obstacle to direct supervision, and is likely to lead to relative independence in practice.

Though it might be suggested that on the basis of their levels of training the workers might be regarded as of 'semi-professional' status,[2] there is a high degree of opportunity for workers who are in the 'front line' to exercise their own professional authority at the expense of the administrative authority of the hierarchy. This tendency is reinforced by the fact that the work places from which the workers commonly operate, particularly the community flats, are buildings extensively used, and in some cases managed by, the consumers of their services. The effect of this is that workers will tend to be influenced by their community contacts. In fact, it is likely that reaction to the way in which workers operate will be more immediate and more direct from consumers than it is from their formal structure of accountability. This tendency will be likely to be reinforced for those workers who identify themselves as accountable to a line manager who is also located in a setting where there is likely to be strong consumer influence. In other words, both supervisor and supervisee are subject to strong direct community influence.

The role of the consumer in community work is not that of passive recipient of service. Rather, community groups exist as a reflection of factors which have motivated their membership to become active, whether this be a housing problem or services for the elderly. The worker may influence what the community comes to see as important but control of the activity lies primarily with community members. The activities of the worker are in this sense, therefore, enabled and sanctioned by the community. Community work is dependent on its consumers to legitimate many of its actions. In this sense there is more organisational permeability than in most other public service occupations. The consumers generally exert a crucial influence over what organisational goals can and will be pursued. This is inherent in the nature of community work, but it is reinforced by the location of practitioners.[3]

The Pattern of Worker Contacts

Turning to the evidence obtained from the workers detailed recordings, the 1983 time-budget analysis of contact activities (presented in Table 3.1 in Chapter 3) begins to give some indication of the range and intensity of contacts with other parties to the community work process. The correlation between the activity analysis material and the network analysis has provided the basis for a time budget of these contacts. This analysis enabled scrutiny from two angles, firstly by exploring the nature of the contacts made within each activity and secondly, by examining the range of activities within which workers had contact with others. It will be helpful to begin, however, with an overall indication of the relative proportions of time that workers spent with the other parties to the community work process.

Table 4.1 (see p. 53) provides a breakdown of the mean percentages of time spent by each type of worker in contact with other groups and combinations of groups, whilst Table 4.2 (see p. 55) indicates the number of workers in each group making contacts of each kind. Comparison of the two Tables provides an indication of both the intensity and extensiveness of contacts of different kinds. It is immediately apparent that two categories stand out as consuming an extensive amount of time. These are contact with other community workers in the social work department, and contact with community group members only. Both were universal activities accounting for an average of 14.8% and 19.7% of work time across the sample as a whole. Notable variations occur, however, between the different groups of workers.

Seniors and Community Development Organisers spent significantly more time on average with other community workers than their Community Worker and Community Work Assistant colleagues. Conversely it is the latter groups which spent substantially more time with the members of community groups. The amount of contact with other community work staff can be seen to have increased with seniority, whilst the amount of contact with community group members decreased with seniority. No doubt this broad pattern reflects the job descriptions of workers in each category.

Table 4.1 Network analysis contacts by group as a percentage of total time
Note: Number of workers recording work in each category in brackets
(W=54)

Category	CWA	CW	SCW	CDO	All
S.W.D. Community Work staff only	11.4(17)	13.7(26)	23.1(5)	22.2(6)	14.8(54)
S.W.D. Community Work and Social Work Staff	2.4(12)	3.7(20)	4.8(5)	5.7(6)	3.6(43)
S.W.D. Social Work staff only	3.4(14)	4.7(24)	4.8(5)	13.5(6)	5.7(49)
Community Education Department staff only	1.8(11)	1.7(21)	2.6(5)	3.8(6)	3.9(43)
Other stat. Community Work staff only	0.5(7)	0.7(8)	- (0)	0.1(1)	0.5(16)
Other stat. non-Community Work staff only	4.4(17)	2.8(22)	2.6(5)	3.8(6)	3.5(50)
Non stat. agency staff only	1.3(16)	1.6(24)	5.1(4)	2.5(6)	1.9(50)
More than 1 stat. or non-stat. agency	0.9(6)	1.5(13)	6.4(4)	3.8(6)	2.0(29)
Community group members only	25.0(17)	21.4(26)	8.2(5)	5.2(6)	19.7(54)
Ordinary members community only	6.3(17)	4.7(21)	1.5(5)	1.2(6)	4.6(49)
Community group and ord. members community	0.5(7)	0.5(7)	- (0)	- (0)	0.4(14)
Politicians only	1.6(8)	0.9(14)	0.3(3)	1.9(6)	1.2(31)
Politicians and community members (gp. and ord.)	0.3(3)	0.5(5)	0.5(1)	- (0)	0.4(9)
CWs and community members	1.9(12)	2.5(16)	0.4(1)	1.2(5)	2.0(34)
CWs, SWs and community members	0.8(6)	0.4(6)	0.5(2)	0.9(3)	0.5(17)
Social workers and community members	1.0(10)	0.2(5)	0.5(1)	0.5(3)	0.6(19)
Community members and other agency staff	3.1(12)	4.2(23)	3.0(5)	2.4(4)	3.6(44)
Politicians and other agency staff	0.3(1)	0.8(8)	- (0)	0.7(2)	0.5(11)
Service staff	0.1(4)	0.4(13)	0.4(3)	0.5(4)	0.2(24)
Unspecified	6.4(16)	7.3(25)	9.0(5)	6.3(6)	7.1(52)
Politicians, other agency and comm. members	- (0)	0.6(4)	2.5(3)	0.7(2)	0.6(9)
Private/commercial agency	0.8(10)	0.7(18)	0.9(4)	0.2(4)	0.7(36)
Paid workers of community groups	1.1(8)	0.8(13)	0.2(1)	1.5(4)	0.9(26)

Key:
CWA = Community Work Assistant CW = Community Worker
SCW = Senior Community Worker CDO = Community Development
Organiser

In rank order of network contacts, in third place came the category of unspecified. By definition this cannot be explored further. It was followed closely by contact with social work staff on their own. In this category the most noticeable feature of the results was the substantially larger proportion of time the Community Development Organisers spent with this group, 13.5% compared with 3.9% for Community Work Assistants and 4.7% for each of the other groups. Contact with social workers was, however, an almost universal activity, recorded by nearly 91% of the sample.

Following this, contact with ordinary members of the community represented 4.6% of contact time overall. Though all Community Development Organisers and Seniors were engaged in this it represented only 1.5% and 1.2% of their time respectively, whereas for the Community Work Assistants and Community Workers (80% of whom were involved), it represented 6.3% and 4.7% of time respectively.

Beyond this point in the rank order no category achieved a score of more than 4%. However, there was still extensive involvement of sample members in the other contacts even though they consumed relatively small amounts of time. There were also a few points at which the patterns for particular worker groups varied substantially from the general pattern. Senior Community Workers, for example, appeared more involved in contacts with non-statutory agencies, and, along with Community Development Organisers, more involved in contacts combining community work and social work staff. In order to take fuller account of the less substantial categories, Table 4.2 has been produced combining categories to indicate the broad patterns in relation to relative levels of contact with other professional workers, community members and politicians. The figures for professional contacts are sub-divided between Social Work Department Community Work staff, other Social Work Department staff and staff of other agencies.

Table 4.2 reinforces the pattern of higher levels of professional contact for more senior workers and relatively higher levels of community contact for more junior workers, though only Community Work Assistants spent more time with the community than professional staff. The table also serves to emphasise the limited levels of contact with politicians.

Table 4.2. Combined network categories by sample group as a percentage of total time

| | Professional Contacts | | | | |
	S.W.D. CW staff	Other S.W.D. staff	Other agency staff	Members of the Community	Politicians
CWA	17.0	8.5	12.4		
		37.9		38.8	2.1
CW	20.3	9.1	13.3		
		42.7		35.2	2.8
SCW	28.4	10.4	19.6		
		58.4		14.4	3.3
CDO	29.6	20.4	15.8		
		65.8		11.3	3.2
All	21.1	10.5	14.4		
		46.1		31.4	2.8

The overall pattern of contacts involved in the workers' activities was probably fairly predictable in that it reflects the role functions of the different designations of workers as set out in the policy document *Helping the Community to Organise*.[4] In it the Director of Social Work comments on the 'direct management and supervision of staff' as the central role of Community Development Organisers and in which they were increasingly supported at the time of the 1983 study by the appointment of Senior Community Workers. Of Community Development Organisers he also stated: 'as a result of the Region's social strategy, the demands of social planning work, including collaborative working with other agencies, have also increased dramatically.'[5] In relation to Seniors he said: 'their appointments have been justified in terms of the unrealistic span of control of Community Development Officers and their primary role is that of staff supervision... Most retain an element of community work practice, and liaise with social work teams and with other agencies locally.'[6]

These role descriptions are entirely consistent with the patterns of how these workers were found to actually spend their time. The community-focused contacts of the other two groups of workers were equally consistent with job descriptions. The basic function of the Community Worker was stated as 'to assist the development of locally relevant forms of community organisation within defined areas of need'.[7] That for Community Work Assistants was 'to assist the community worker(s) in the achievement of tasks within designated areas'.[8]

By 1989 the only apparent change in these overall patterns related to the role of the Senior which, in the absence of Community Development Organisers, had taken on more social planning functions (ironically raising the complaint that their span of responsibility like that formerly undertaken by Community Development Organisers had become too wide!).

Finally this chapter explores the nature of the contacts between community workers and politicians, other professional workers and members of the community. In doing so, consideration will be given to the activity contexts identified in Chapter 3, in which these contacts most frequently occurred.

Contacts with Politicians

Since much of this contact time appears to represent occasions where workers happened to be in the same place at the same time as politicians, rather than being in direct communication, the picture of a low level of significant contact is reinforced. Taking the four categories for contact with politicians, the most significant was contact with politicians alone represented just over one-third of these contacts, though the proportion for Community Development Organisers was 55%. Taken in the light of the often negative views of workers about the understanding that they believe politicians have of the nature of community work (see Chapter 7), the apparent lack of attention to improving their understanding is curious. Similarly, the very small amount of time (see Table 3.3) spent at District or Regional Council meetings suggests a lack of direct monitoring of the political component of the policy-making process.

Contacts with other Professional Workers

Examining the professional contacts of the workers it is helpful to continue to draw the distinction between Social Work Department community work staff, other Social Work Department staff and staff of other agencies. Workers spent 21.1% of their contact time with other community workers, 14.9% being with them alone and most of the remainder in combination with other professional workers. Overall, time with other Social Work Department community workers increased substantially with seniority. The ratio of un-planned to planned contact time was much higher for Community Work Assistants and Community Workers than the most senior groups. The chance nature of much contact may lead to questions about its purposefulness.

Turning to the patterns of contact with other social work staff, Community Development Organisers had substantially more contact in this category than their colleagues (20.4% of contact time compared with an overall mean for the sample of 10.5%). For all groups, contact with other social work staff was primarily an inter-professional activity (that is, it excluded contact with community members or other persons) and for all groups the contact was more likely to be only with other social work staff. Again, the likelihood of the contact being unplanned decreased with seniority.

As the discussion of the content of workers activities in Chapter 3 showed, the contacts of more senior staff with members of their own department also tended to involve managerial functions.

As later discussion shows (see Chapter 6), many workers held generally negative attitudes to their employing department, and generally did not value their contacts with their social work colleagues.

In relation to the pattern of contacts with other agencies, though 14.5% of contact time was spent with these workers, it should be noted that a wide variety of agencies was involved. Overall, 68% of time spent with other agencies was solely with other professional workers and this rose to over 75% for the two more senior groups. Contact with Community Education Department workers was not extensive though its level rose with seniority. Over half of these contacts occurred in the other pre-planned category indicating that they had specific purposes but tended not to be part of on-going interactions. The level of pre-planned contact again rose with seniority. At a field level, contact with community education staff was as likely to be incidental as planned.

The results indicate that contact with other statutory agencies (other than community work ones) were with service departments of local, or central government and for specific purposes rather than part of an on-going programme of contacts. They accounted for 3.4% of time.

Contacts with another agency in combination with members of the community accounted for 3.5% of contact time. It appears that the involvement of these agencies in community group meetings was an occasional rather than a regular feature of their activities.

Contacts with the Community

Whilst overall 31.4% of time was spent with members of the community, the variations between the worker groups were substantial. Community Development Organisers and Senior Community Workers spent just 11.9% and 16.9% of contact time respectively compared with 35.2% and 38.8% for Community Workers and Community Work Assistants. Approximately 60% of community contact time was spent with community group members excluding contact with other groups and the most common context was non-statutory, non-social group meetings. Community Development Organisers spent the highest proportion of their time with community groups members in the formal meetings of their groups. The other three groups were all much more involved in unplanned contacts. Contacts with ordinary members of the community, as against members of community groups, represented just 4.5% of time compared with 19.2% for the latter. This suggests that most community work staff maintained fairly regular contact with a limited number of people active in their communities rather than having contacts with a wide range of community members. Given that the most common context for these contacts was the category of unplanned contact, this implication is further reinforced.

Of the combination categories involving community members, the most common at 3.5% of time overall was contact with community members and other agencies. Approximately half of these contacts took place in community group meetings and a further third were in the other pre-planned category.

Comment on Patterns of Contact

It has already been noted that the general patterns of time spent in contact with the other parties to the community work process by each designation of worker was highly consistent with their job descriptions. In this sense the findings are also unsurprising when broken down in more detail in relation to particular categories of activity. They do, however, reinforce the comments made in relation to the findings on the location of the workers, for they indicate clearly that the Community Workers and Community Work Assistants carried the primary role as field-workers, and that in carrying this role, they were substantially more organisationally distanced from their sponsoring agency than the Seniors and Community Development Organisers. The influence of the community contacts in the unplanned areas of activity demonstrates the 'front line' nature of their location as does the extensiveness of community contacts in the non-statutory group meetings.

The fieldworkers' pattern of contacts provides a basis for understanding why workers often express frustrations over the role strains that they experience in community work. On the one hand they feel subject to the bureaucratic authority of their employers, whilst on the other they feel a sense of loyalty to the communities with whom they are engaged in attempts to resolve problems. This is a tension that has been endemic to community work, though community workers should guard against the illusion that their occupation is unique in this regard. Teachers, for example, who wish to respond to educational needs as defined by students, may be constrained by the demands of a pre-formed curriculum. The tension between loyalty and accountability is nonetheless a central dilemma for community work and this is demonstrated by the comments given by these respondents about their work which are discussed in the following Chapters.

It is often presumed that the role strain experienced by community workers reflects a tension between radical worker aspirations and conservative employment agencies. Certainly this is not unusual as the history of the Home Office Community Development Projects[9] illustrated, but the tension can arise for other reasons, not least the radical expectations of employers placed on workers who operate with conservative communities. Often the tension is about the pace of change. Sponsors may expect concrete results in short timescales because they fail to recognise the difficulties involved in generating activity in communities which may have reached a point of conditioned helplessness as a result of the persistent intractability of the problems they face. In this regard the low level of planned and purposeful contact which Community Workers and Community Work Assistants appear to have had with politicians is of concern in that a more active dialogue might reduce the degree to which conflict is experienced.

It is important to acknowledge that Strathclyde Region does recognise these problems in its policy statements on community work, though the meaning of some of the statements remains ambiguous until tested in specific situations. In its policy review of community work in 1978, for example, it stated that 'each community worker has to make his own honest decision about how he maintains loyalty to his employer, loyalty to the community in which he works and his own self respect' and later that those selecting community workers should 'attempt to ensure that those selected are mature enough in philosophy to challenge the system while living within its constraints'.[10]

The simultaneous pressures of community and sponsors' interests indicate the importance for community workers of good communication, negotiation, brokerage and advocacy skills and the need for qualities of resilience, tenacity, patience, self-reliance and openness. Community workers, even if they spend little time in direct contact with politicians, operate constantly in a politically dynamic environment.

The comment, so far, has concentrated on the position of the more field-oriented staff, but it is also the case that line managers of community workers may experience some of the same tensions, though from a different position. If they are to carry their managerial and supervisory functions effectively, they must do so with full recognition of the dilemmas which face those whom they supervise. Thus, though they may spend much higher proportions of their time working with their community work and social work colleagues, many of the same accountability and loyalty issues arise. These are likely to be exacerbated where they are expected to carry social planning functions which are based as much on normative or comparative definitions of need as the expressed needs of the communities affected. Thus they may manage workers whose reference points for defining appropriate action may not necessarily be compatible with their own.

Notes

1. G. Smith, *Social Work and the Sociology of Organisations* (London: Routledge and Kegan Paul, 1970) pp. 36–43.
2. A. Etzioni, *The Semi-professions and their Organisation – Teachers, Nurses, Social Workers* (New York: The Free Press, 1969).

3. See for example, *Consumers Guide to Community Work* (London: Association of Community Workers with National Consumer Council, 1987).
4. Director of Social Work, *Helping the Community to Organise* (Strathclyde Regional Council, 1984).
5. Ibid. para. 9.2.
6. Ibid. para. 9.4.
7. Ibid. App. 3.
8. Ibid.
9. For a discussion of the CDP Programme, see for example M. Loney, *Community Against Government* (London: Heinemann Educational Books, 1983).
10. A. Worthington, *Policy Review Group on Community Development Services* ('the Worthington Report') (Strathclyde Regional Council, 1978) pp. 12–13.

Part III
Workers' Views on their Practice

5

Community Workers' Aspirations for, and Evaluation of, their Work

Introduction

Whilst so far we have concentrated on the evidence in relation to the work that community workers actually do, it is of equal importance to understand what it is that they wish to achieve, and how they evaluate the work they do relative to these aspirations. The preceding discussion provides a basis for assessing whether what workers spend their time doing fulfils their aspirations and whether there is any dissonance between how time is actually used and the ways in which workers might wish to use it. To use the words of Harry Specht,[1] are community workers activities characterised by 'large hopes but small realities'?

In order to explore these questions, the evidence on which this Chapter is based is drawn from the answers given by respondents to three questions in the 1983 study. The first asked: 'What do you hope your community work will achieve?' The question was deliberately located at the beginning of the follow-up interview to ensure that the workers were free to comment openly and without influence from reflection on the actual work undertaken in the recorded month (such reflection was a requirement of later questions).

Whereas the first question explored aspirations in the abstract, the other two concentrated on exploration of the work that the respondents had actually recorded. The first part asked them to reflect on this work and consider: 'What aspects of your work during the recorded month do you value most highly in relation to the objectives identified in question 1?' The second asked them to identify those which they valued least.

In addition to exploring the aspirations for and evaluations of their own work, the research also explored the practice models of community work with which the workers most closely identified. They were asked to identify from the following list the model with which they would most readily associate themselves: adult education, community care, community action, social planning, community development, neighbourhood work and community organisation. Further, the workers were asked to identify the characteristics which they most closely associated with their preferred model. On this basis it was possible to see how closely their perceptions of models were associated with textbook precepts.

For the purposes of analysing these questions, comments recorded from interviews were categorised into qualitative groups, quantified and rank ordered as a proportion of comments made. The overall rank order was contrasted with the rank orders for each group in the sample and on the basis of age (contrasting those above and below the mean age of 32 years), sex, professional qualification (comparing CQSW holders with all other qualified staff) and work location (comparing those who shared an office base with other social work staff with those who did not).

Workers Aspirations

Considering what the workers hoped their work would achieve, there was very little variation in response between the sample strata. The most popular comment category focused on 'the identification of local issues and promotion of organisations of the community to make their own responses and achieve change. In so doing to increase the confidence, self esteem, independence, knowledge and skill of local community members.' This might be offered as a definition of classical community development work. It emphasises the role of the worker in promoting organisational mechanisms within the community by which it may address its problems and move into a self-sustaining process of change and development based on the growth of confidence and knowledge in community groups.

The second category, though similar to the first, is distinguished from it by its emphasis on personal growth of individual community members which enables them as individuals rather than as members of community groups to tackle their problems more effectively. It reads: 'spread skills, knowledge, information and self belief to individuals in the locality to assist them in relating to the system, facing their problems, participating in decisions, obtaining their rights.'

The third category borrows from the first two but here the emphasis is on establishing control over events rather than simply influencing them. In other words, it is a variation in degree rather than direction. Comments in this category relate both to control by people of their own lives and collectively over the life of the communities of which they are part. Typical phrases employed were 'promote local control/self sufficiency/self determination by people in relation to their own lives and communities'.

The next most popular cluster of comments formed a composite group containing a range of rather general aspirations for improved conditions in the communities in which the workers operate. Their binding feature is their generality combined with lack of reference to the process by which these ends will be achieved.

Further comments in the rank order continued to give emphasis to change within the neighbourhoods in which workers operated. Only a few of the sample referred explicitly in their comments to developing political awareness of the nature and causes of problems, though this is implicit in the third ranked category noted above. Other comments focused on the importance of helping agencies which deliver services, or have potential influence over events in the area, to understand community issues; promotion of caring services; and on community work as a strategy designed to achieve resource redistribution to disadvantaged communities.

Since most workers made several comments it is important to recognise that theoretical eclecticism was not uncommon among these workers. Nonetheless it is useful to compare their general tenor with the models of practice with which workers associated themselves.

Overall, the workers placed an extremely heavy emphasis on changes within the communities in which they worked (73.6% of the comments made focused in this way, whereas 14.4%

focused on change in the outlook and practices of public service agencies).

There were some significant variations in value stance which are implicit in the comments. A breakdown of the comment categories into those reflecting radical, moderate and conservative orientations towards community work practice indicates that 16% could be said to have associated with the radical or community action school, 51% with the more moderate or community development school and 7% with the conservative community care/integration school. The remainder are not readily identified with particular stances.[2]

In relation to the preferences expressed by the workers between different practice models, these results are generally consistent. Overall, 39% associated themselves with the community development approach. 20% of the sample identified themselves primarily with the community action model whilst 9% identified with community care. The characteristics which the workers associated with these models were readily compatible with their usage in community work literature. A further 13% identified with the term neighbourhood work. This was seen primarily as defining the place rather than style of work but comments suggest that these workers would be divided between community development and community care styles. Only one worker specifically identified with adult education as his primary model of practice. However, it should be noted that community development was seen as encompassing personal learning processes for participants which is consistent with the high proportion of workers identifying this as an aspiration for their practice.

This pattern of distribution of aspirations for their work is of particular interest when related back to the actual nature of their practice as described in Chapter 3 and the pattern of work contacts as described in Chapter 4. In relation to the content of their work, the workers hopes do not seem to have been grossly unrelated to the realities of their practice. The emphasis in practice on resource work and the provision of community premises, facilities and amenities can be seen as related to the objectives of neighbourhood community development indicated by the above analysis. The low level of campaigning work identified from the workers recordings would also appear to correlate with the relatively low level of radical aspirations. The limited emphasis on engagement with local authority policy processes also seems to be consistent with the relatively low level of aspiration to influence the local authority, especially the Social Work Department.

Considering the contact networks involved in their activities, the extensive levels of contact with members of the community, particularly community group members, among Community Work Assistant and Community Workers, also appears to have been consistent with the community-focused aspirations for their work. Though contact with other professional workers was actually greater in terms of time, later material on the ways in which workers valued these contacts will suggest that they were much less significant to the workers.

There were few differences related to age, sex, work location or qualifications.

Workers Evaluations

Positive Aspects

Taking those aspects of their work during the month which they had valued most highly first, overall the most common category was work with community groups. Interestingly, this reflects the actual pattern of contacts in the network analysis of worker recordings. Overall, 41.6% of comments related to work with community groups and 22.2% to work with other professionals. In the former group of categories, it is interesting that almost half the comments seem to be as concerned with the process of group support itself as with the specific tasks which their activities were designed to accomplish. This suggests that non-directive stances towards community groups were highly valued. That work with networks or forums of community groups formed the third most valued category, is in contrast with the parochial orientations thought to be held by community groups themselves (see Chapter 8). This type of work was not extensively reflected in worker recordings. Where the focus of work with groups was specified, housing campaigns were particularly valued. In fifth place in the rank order of categories came community care schemes and corporate working. They were followed by intermediate treatment/youth and children's work; advice and information work; and work with the unemployed.

Overall, the results produce a slightly confusing picture; however, when examined by worker groups, the pattern becomes more clear. Similarities appear between Community Development Organisers and Senior Community Workers compared with the other two groups. They valued work with community development colleagues and corporate working particularly highly. Community Development Organisers also appeared to value work with management highly. Community Workers were characterised by valuing direct contact with community groups most highly whereas by contrast Community Work Assistants valued service provision work more highly. Their placing of community care, intermediate treatment/youth and children's work, and advice and information work in the first three places, reinforces the picture emerging from the recordings of Community Work Assistants and Community Workers having contrasting orientations to their work, the former being more service-oriented and the latter more issue-oriented. Women, probably as a result of their higher proportion among Community Work Assistants and CQSW trained staff, valued community care activities more highly than their colleagues.

The results of the question examining the practice models with which workers most closely identify are generally compatible with these results.

Negative Aspects

Turning to the aspects of their work that the respondents valued least highly during the recorded month, it is perhaps predictable that administration should be the most common category. However, it is interesting in that it did not prove to be a very extensive activity in the time budgets of the workers. Another non-contact activity – written work, report preparation and recording – came in second place. Admittedly half of the comments related to the recording for the research project which is understandable, but its general ranking, given that it again was a relatively insubstantial aspect of the time budgets, is of note. Work with other community development staff was in third place alongside work with other social work colleagues and work with social work management. Given the views expressed about social work management attitudes to community work, discussed in Chapter 6, the latter two categories may be understandable; however, work with other community development staff was also ranked the second most valued activity by the workers and was the second largest contact category in the network analysis. Its low ranking here was largely a reflection of the view of Community Work Assistants.

Other negatively valued aspects of work were corporate working, 'odd obligements', information and advice work and in-service training.

Examined by sample strata, the results in relation to least-valued activities show most variation for Community Work Assistants who expressed little frustration with administration but a substantial level of frustration with work with community development colleagues. Low value was attached by Community Workers, in particular, to work with social work colleagues. Women appeared frustrated by 'odd obligements' and corporate working. Younger workers were more frustrated by work with social work colleagues, older workers by corporate working. Being located away from other social work staff appeared to reduce levels of frustration with social work management. Having a social work qualification, however, seemed not to be significantly influential in terms of relationships with social work colleagues or social work management.

Concluding Comment

If a broad conclusion were to be drawn from the material on worker aspirations it would be that they associate themselves primarily with reformist styles of community work practice. Community development emerges not only as a preferred model but also as the one which most adequately describes the largest proportion of work being undertaken. The American writers Kramer and Specht[3] argue that community development is concerned with 'efforts to mobilise the people who are affected by a community condition... into groups and organisations to enable them to take action on these social problems and issues which affect them'.

Clearly, such enabling functions are emphasised in the aspirations of the sample of workers described in this study. They might more readily identify themselves, however, with a definition of community development drawn from British literature. Thomas[4] argues that: 'the community development strategy emphasises self help, mutual support, the building up of neighbourhood integration, the development of neighbourhood capacities for problem solving and self representation, and the

promotion of collective action to bring the community's preferences to the attention of political decision makers'.

Such an approach does not appear incompatible with the
aspirations for community work expressed in the policy statements of Strathclyde Regional Council and its Social Work
Department in particular (discussed in Chapter 1). Yet material
in the following chapters will nonetheless show that there is
considerable tension between the community work staff and
both their managers and the politicians with responsibility for
their activities. If the primary practice model had been a community action one, such conflict might have been anticipated.
Perlman and Gurin[5] describe this approach thus: 'The goal is
change in power relationships and resources. The clientele are
disadvantaged segments of the community and the practice is
one of helping them to become organised, to crystallise action
issues, and to engage in conflict oriented action against the
power structure.'

This conflictual and confrontational approach did not predominate yet the frustrations of workers were clearly expressed.
It should not be assumed therefore that the conflict can be
explained as a clash between radical worker aspiration and a
conservative policy framework.

Notes

1. H. Specht, 'The Dilemmas of Community Work in the UK', *Policy
    and Politics*, vol. 4, no. 1 (1975) p. 65.
2. For a discussion of such models, see for example A. Barr,
    'Practice Models and Training Issues' in L. Bidwell and C.
    McConnell, *Community Education and Community Development*
    (Dundee College of Education, 1982).
3. R.M. Kramer and H. Specht (eds), *Readings in Community
    Organisation Practice* (Englewood Cliffs, New Jersey: Prentice
    Hall, 1969) p. 10.
4. D.N. Thomas, *The Making of Community Work* (London: George
    Allen and Unwin, 1983) p. 109.
5. R. Perlman and A. Gurin, *Community Organisation and Social
    Planning* (New York: John Wiley and Son, 1972) p. 55.

6

Community Workers and their Managers

Introduction

Community work is an activity which is generally located in a variety of host organisations with much broader overall purposes. Though there have been developments of agencies specifically focused on community work, this is uncommon in local authorities. In Strathclyde, when the community development and deprivation strategies were being planned, there was considerable debate as to whether there should be a department of community work. This approach was not adopted, although a separate Community Development Committee concerned with this activity within the host departments (particularly Education and Social Work) was established. One of the consequences of this decision in the Social Work Department was that community workers were ultimately managed by staff who generally lacked experience or substantial knowledge of community work. Though a Regional Community Development Organiser was appointed, the organisational structure of the department left him in an advisory role whilst the community work staff was managed through the hierarchy of the five social work divisions.

Given the extensiveness of community work employment in other host departments, the problems of non-specialist management are of general interest, though these findings are particularly pertinent to social work and social services departments with significant numbers of community work staff. They are also of relevance in considering the breadth of training which may be required if non-specialist departments are to be effective hosts to community work. Conversely, the findings indicate the importance of a general understanding of the host setting among the specialist workers. This again has implications for training, both pre-service and in-service.

The range of such non-specialist departments is potentially very wide. Strathclyde Region employs community development workers not just in Social Work but also in its Education and Chief Executive's Departments. In other councils such staff may be found in Housing, Leisure and Recreation, Libraries, Economic Development, Environmental Health, Planning and other departments.

Since the research only examined the attitudes of community work staff and not other members of their departments, the evidence can only explore their perceptions of their managers. How reasonable these attitudes may be is a matter for conjecture; however, in that they reflect what community work staff feel, they do represent one side of the management equation.

The evidence in this Chapter is drawn primarily from the response given by respondents to two questions from the 1983 study . The first asked workers: 'What do you think Strathclyde Regional Council Social Work Department [that is, the Senior Management] hope your community work will achieve?' The second related specifically to the work that the respondents had undertaken in the recorded month and asked them to indicate what they thought their managers would regard as the most and least valuable aspects of their community work relative to the objectives identified in answer to the first question.

The procedures for analysis of this data were the same as those adopted for the material discussed in the previous chapter. Recorded comments were categorised into qualitative groups, quantified and rank ordered as a proportion of the comments made.

As in the previous chapter, the overall rank ordering of comments was contrasted with the rank orders not only of each strata of the sample but also in relation to age (contrasting those above and below the mean age of 32 years), sex, professional qualification (comparing CQSW holders with all other qualified workers), and work location (comparing those sharing an office base with other social work staff with those who do not).

Workers' Views of the Aspirations of their Senior Managers

Exploring the general views as to the expectations of their social work managers, the overriding characteristic is the negativity of the comments of the workers. The most popular category reflected a feeling that social work management would wish to impose limitations on the scope of their workers' activity which directly linked them to a client, rather than a more general community focus. In turn, this produced a sense of second-class status among community workers relative to their social work colleagues. The comments form a composite category; collectively they revealed a sense of frustration about the kinds of activities which the workers felt to be valued. The workers' comments should not necessarily be interpreted as devaluing service-based or client-focused work per se, but rather as rejecting an approach to community work which sees it merely as a subservient service function to mainstream social work activities. The tenor of feeling is well illustrated by the following example: 'Social work management see community work as secondary to social work, to be tolerated only if concerned with respectable groups (for example playgroups, leisure groups)'.

Of the two sets of comments in second place, one was more conciliatory in tone whilst the other was highly negative about social work management. The former was in many ways similar to the first group, particularly in its emphasis on the value attached by social work management to community care and preventive strategies. However, the tone of these comments revealed a greater level of shared values between social work management and the community workers making the comments. The workers acknowledged a genuine concern on the part of social work management to see their efforts produce resolution to local problems though through adoption of a generally conservative style of community work activity. Hence comments like 'community workers are expected to adopt a preventive community care approach and to develop the use of volunteers and self-help'.

These comments are interesting to compare with those in the other group like 'social work management do not appreciate or understand what community work can do/are not committed to community work/are not interested in community efforts'. These represented a highly negative comment by the workers on the attitudes of their management which really questioned their level of commitment to community work as an activity. That over a fifth of the workers should have been so lacking in confidence in the support, knowledge or interest of their senior social work management is disturbing.

Two categories of comment also tied for fourth place in the rank order. Again they contrasted markedly in their negative and positive orientations. The first was one of the most positive reflecting a belief in the commitment of senior management to the role of community work as an anti-deprivation strategy. One worker said, for example: 'Social work management hope community work will lead to an increased level of community activity directed towards local issues in deprived areas leading to changes at local level.'

The other fourth-ranked category, however, returned to a negative stance. Here the workers claimed that the level of communication with senior management was of such poor quality that the workers did not know what management hoped would be achieved by the employment of community workers.

In the smaller remaining comment categories there continued to be ambivalence in the comments made. Some acknowledged a willingness on the part of the Social Work Department to be influenced by and learn from community initiatives, whilst others saw the department's motives as suspect. There was acknowledgement too that the experience varied considerably between managers who appreciated the nature of community work and those who did not.

There were few differences in outlook between the four worker groups. Of more interest was the overall distribution of comments between those which could be regarded as relatively negative, relatively positive or neutral about the aspirations of social work managers for the work of their community workers.

Analysis of the comment categories by this means revealed the level of negative feeling about the views of senior social work management among community work staff generally and some variation between the strata. The pattern revealed was one of substantial negative views, (50.5%), relative to positive views (31.2%), for the sample as a whole, with this pattern accentuated for the Community Worker and Community Development Organiser groups. Only among the Senior Community Workers were negative comments balanced by positive ones. These results raise interesting questions about whether community development staff are appropriately located in the Social Work Department. They are totally consistent with the valuation given to work with social work management in the exploration of the aspects of their work which the workers had valued themselves (see Chapter 5).

Examination of these results in relation to the variables of age, sex, qualification and work location produces little variation in relative rank ordering of comments except in relation to the last. Workers not sharing their office base with other social work staff showed a markedly lower degree of frustration about the aspirations of their senior managers.

It may be suggested that the findings in relation to work location indicate less difficulty in their relationships with the social work department, particularly its managers. The impression is left that these workers may have had a relatively higher degree of operational autonomy but that as a consequence they were more able to see themselves as promoting activities which would be valued by their managers and took a much more optimistic view of the potential congruence of objectives between their managers and themselves. Conversely, it suggests that workers located alongside other social work staff, and hence directly subject to the expression of social work values, were more conscious of differences between their own objectives and those of social work as a whole. Workers operating independently of other social work staff may have been more able to fulfil their own work objectives than their colleagues who felt constrained by the influences and expectations of mainstream social work. Though this evidence relates directly only to community work in a social work department, it is possible that proximity to the mainstream workers of any host department in which community workers are based may increase the degree of role strain which they experience.

In relation to the other variables, it is worth noting that CQSW holders were more negative about the quality of communication with their senior managers than those holding other professional qualifications. This may reflect their higher level of expectation that community work would be understood by their managers, based on having a common experience of training with other social work staff. This finding is the reverse of the conclusion of the Thomas and Warburton study[1] which suggested that those trained in social work were better integrated into their host department.

Workers' Evaluation of their Practice Relative to the Ascribed Aspirations of their Managers.

Positive Aspects

The views of workers when examining the actual work they had undertaken during the recorded month were generally compatible with their views of their managers' general aspirations for community work. The workers believed that their most commonly valued activity was in relation to community care and services schemes. Also thought to be valued were work with social work colleagues and advice and information work, which shared equal second place in the rank order. Some seemed to think the former was valued because it involved support to social workers in activities related to traditional client groups and others since it might promote greater awareness of the nature of community work. Advice and information work may partly have been cited because it reflects a more individualised client orientation more readily understandable to social work managers. Other categories thought to be valued were work with other community development staff; work with unemployed; corporate working; work with social work management; general work with community groups; intermediate treatment/youth and children's work; and resource work.

There are some interesting variations between the strata of the sample. Community Development Organisers and Senior Community Workers emphasised tasks related to their managerial roles. Work with social work management and work with other community development staff were particularly popular categories. Senior Community Workers also stressed corporate working. Community Workers and Community Work Assistants emphasised direct work within the community, especially community care and service work, and information and advice work.

In relation to aspects of work thought to be valued by social work management, workers located independent of other social work staff placed less emphasis on work with colleagues and their managers and more on corporate working. Non-CQSW staff believed that community care was more highly valued than their colleagues.

Negative Aspects

In relation to those aspects of their work that it was felt the managers of the Social Work Department would not value, workers identified housing campaigns most commonly. The implication is that their managers did not value the style of work involved and this view is reinforced by two of the three categories in equal second place in the rank order. One was unspecified work which challenges the local authority, and the other was work with the unemployed. The negative view of the former is self-evident whilst for the latter, it is again the style of approach which seems to have been of concern. Workers suggested that the activity was 'conceptually difficult to relate to social work' and unpopular because it was 'issue based'. The concern that social work managers would not value work to provide community premises, facilities and amenities is more difficult to understand. Concern seems to have been over the time and expense involved and that the activity may be seen as rather trivial. Other not uncommonly cited categories were corporate working; administrative and clerical work; 'odd obligements'; informal discussions; and work with individuals and families.

Variations appeared in relation to whether workers were located alongside social work colleagues or not. The latter group showed less concern about more radical campaigning styles of work and more concern about corporate working.

Comment

If we were to draw a general conclusion from this evidence, it would be that the relationship between the community work staff as a whole and their host department was a difficult one. It can be argued that the nature of community work itself, when it is concerned with the promotion of active community participation in local affairs and criticism of policies, is problematic to any sponsoring agent. But the problems here seemed to lie much deeper. The evidence only provided insight into the way community work staff saw the problems but it appears that they believed there to be fundamental differences of value between community work and social work. Some appeared much more alienated from the predominant culture and ideology of social work than others but the extent of the negativity when compared with the evidence from Chapter 5 that most workers appeared to adopt a quite moderate stance in relation to community work, suggests a significant problem. The evidence in Chapter 4 indicates that most workers had quite substantial contact with social work colleagues and cannot therefore be regarded as likely to have been operating solely on the basis of myths that they projected about social workers. There was a strong feeling that social workers generally, and their managers in particular, lacked a real understanding of community work and possibly a commitment to it. Given that the work undertaken, as described in Chapter 5, was generally non-controversial and fitted quite well with the philosophy of practice outlined in the Social Work Director's review of community work of 1984,[2] discussed in Chapter 1, the sources of the cultural and ideological differences are worthy of examination. Unfortunately this research did not explore these dimensions on a comparative basis; however, one of the factors which may have bearing was the very low number of workers who held qualifications in social work as revealed in the analysis in Chapter 2. Just 29% were qualified in social work.

The influence of qualifications on workers attitudes to employment in a social work department was also discussed by Thomas and Warburton. They distinguished between 'endogenous workers' – those oriented towards a social work culture – and 'exogenous workers' – those oriented in other directions – and indicated that the former were more likely to have social work training. They found that the endogenous workers 'seemed able better to manage the simultaneous roles of colleague and internal change agent... and that of the external change agent in the community'.[3]

The analysis of responses relative to qualification in this sample however, indicates a greater level of frustration by those holding social work qualifications than among their non-social work qualified colleagues. This finding could be indicative of different expectations in the two groups of the attitudes that they would expect to find in their host department. In the decade since the Thomas and Warburton study there had been increasingly heavy emphasis in social work training on 'unitary methods', that is, an approach to social work practice involving case, group and community work methods. Those trained in such a framework but finding that it did not seem to have extensively influenced social work practice may have been particularly aggrieved by what they may perceived as the devaluing of the contribution of community work.

It is also relevant to ask from what background social work managers are drawn. No detailed information on this is available for Strathclyde. Though it is known that there was one divisional director and one district manager from a community work background at the time of the research, the vast majority of managers would have been likely to be social work trained, and, given their age, to have studied at a time prior to significant influence of community work on social work training.

Many of these issues were also recognised in the Crousaz and Davies[4] research. They reported that 'communication with the wider department, the senior management or other area officers was not always easy for an area office community worker ... area officers were not themselves generally trained or experienced in community work'. Crousaz and Davies also reported difficulty for community workers engaging the interest of social workers. So too did Stevenson and Parsloe (1978).[5] Their study covered 31 social work teams including 225 respondents of whom just 7 were community workers. They found no examples of 'social workers deliberately attempting to develop community work as an alternative mode of intervention, unless they were in a designated specialist post'.[6] They also said: 'these findings suggest that the vast majority of team members were not practising a generic approach with regard to methods of intervention. The Seebohm report sounds a little hollow.'[7] Elsewhere, Stevenson comments in relation to community workers: 'our research showed the discomfort experienced by the handful of such workers whom we found in the thirty-one area teams studied.'[8]

These findings of other studies offer parallel evidence of difficulties encountered by community work in social work settings. The findings for Strathclyde may not therefore be exceptional. It is, of course, difficult to gauge the degree of the difficulties relative to those which many occupational groups may record in relation to bureaucratic organisational and managerial questions. Payne, for example, reviewing research findings on job satisfaction in social work, lists commonly expressed dissatisfaction as 'resources, work pressure, absence of a career grade, the various aspects of the organisations (size, bureaucracy) and management'.[9]

Whilst this research was undertaken in relation to community workers in a social work department, it would be unreasonable to suppose that the problems identified are particular to that setting. The research studies by Cliffe,[10] on community work in Leicester, and Davies and Crousaz[11] of community work in London Boroughs both included substantial proportions of their samples from both the voluntary sector and local authority departments other than social work. Both reported that very few line managers of community work had substantial experience in the field. Davies and Crousaz state that: 'in most departments the supervision available to even the most inexperienced community worker was very limited'.[12]

Cliffe records 62% of his sample as dissatisfied with support and supervision available to them. Though the dissatisfaction was widespread, the social services department was not the most heavily criticised. Cliffe concludes in relation to all the employment settings: 'the sheer volume of complaints about inadequate support and supervision suggests that the problem is real and urgent.'[13]

Both of these studies identified lack of understanding of community work as a critical factor in the supervisory and managerial relationships. Since these problems appear to be widespread amongst all community work employers, the central lessons may have more to do with the nature of community work, with its emphasis on empowering consumer organisations, than with the particular nature of social work. If the host organisation, whether it is an education, social work, chief executive's or other local authority department, is itself open to dialogue with community interests and adopts practices which are empowering rather than controlling, it is likely that internal organisational tensions will be reduced. Indeed the evidence from this research is that there appeared to be great differences in relationships between workers and managers related to the degree of congruence of their value framework and consequent practices.

The conclusion from this must be that any local authority department which sponsors community work should behave in relation to all its activities in a manner which is consistent with empowering and enabling community organisations to participate and have influence. Thus, local authority departments wishing to take this approach cannot do so without ensuring that these principles permeate all their activities. Anything less than this promotes contradictions in behaviour of different categories of worker and legitimates allegations that community work is a token gesture, a sop to the notion of consumer sovereignty. It would be unfair, however, to suggest that Strathclyde Regional Council, or its Social Work Department in particular, have not recognised these difficulties. Indeed it aspires to a community development perspective in all its practices. What is apparent, however, is that stating such an intention is much more straightforward than producing the desired outcome.

It is a naive community worker, however, who does not expect to encounter these difficulties. In the case of Strathclyde Social Work Department it is not unreasonable to suggest that such naivety was commonplace in 1983 and that community workers themselves needed to be more sophisticated and systematic in their presentation of their practice and their attempts to achieve wider influence in their organisations.

In the light of these comments it is pleasing to be able to report that the audit of community workers undertaken in 1989 revealed an improving picture.

Comparison with the 1989 Audit

Analysis reveals that there is a continuing ambivalence amongst workers about their relationship with social work but that there are many more positive features of the relationship than in 1983.

Workers were invited to identify up to five factors in relation to community work to which attention needed to be given. The most substantial areas of concern were to do with resourcing of local community work processes and frustration about inadequate training and career development opportunity. Almost all workers commented on these factors, however less than half commented on relationships within the social work department and only a third directly related to managerial concerns. A sizeable number of workers still felt that community work was marginalised and of low status within the social work department, that the quality of managerial support and understanding was poor and that there was a general lack of commitment to community work. However, in meetings with the community work teams there was substantial evidence of positive and improving relationships in many parts of the Region. There was an almost equal balance between teams of workers reporting favourably on the support and responsiveness of the District Management Team and those reporting unfavourably. Similarly in terms of relationships with area team managers, teams were equally divided.

It would be misleading to describe this as a transformation but it is a remarkable shift from the substantially negative views of 1983. Several explanations are possible. Firstly, the former Community Development Organisers have become important figures in management at district and area team levels. They have infused a community development perspective which has created a better climate in which community work can operate. It is very noticeable that the level of frustration and criticism correlates broadly with those district management teams and area teams without managers experienced in and knowledgeable about community work. Secondly, the restructuring of the Social Work Department in 1986 brought community work directly into the area team line management structure. At the time, most community work staff were very critical of this fearing that they would lose their identity and be pressured into a primary orientation to social work client group concerns. Whilst there are teams who have felt that this has been the case, it is not a majority experience. Relationships are at their most positive where area teams have adopted a neighbourhood-based community social work approach. Generally in these settings, community work has found valuable collaborative roles with social workers but has not felt that its distinct functions and priorities have been eroded. On the contrary, better understanding from social work has legitimised its role. Thirdly, it may simply be that the diffusion of innovation is a long-term process and the improved relationship is merely a reflection of the pace at which the role of community work has come to be appreciated. Thus, even in social work area teams not operating on a community social work model, workers increasingly report good collaboration on specific issues.

Notes

1.   D.N. Thomas and R.W. Warburton, *Community Workers in Social Service Departments: a Case Study* (London: National Institute for Social Work, 1977).

2.   Director of Social Work, *Helping the Community to Organise* (Strathclyde Regional Council, 1984).

3.   Thomas and Warburton, *Community Workers*, p. 11.

4. C. Davies and D. Crousaz, *Local Authority Community Work – Realities of Practice* (London: HMSO, 1982) p. 24.
5. O. Stevenson and P. Parsloe, *Social Service Teams: The Practitioner's View* (London: HMSO, 1978).
6. Ibid. p.134.
7. Ibid. p. 131.
8. O. Stevenson, *Specialisation in Social Service Teams* (London: George Allen and Unwin, 1981) p. 120.
9. D. Payne, 'Job Satisfaction and Social Work' in J. Lishman, *Social Work Departments as Organisations*, Research Highlights No. 4. (University of Aberdeen, 1984) p. 63.
10. D. Cliffe, *Community Work in Leicester* (Leicester: Centre for Mass Communication Research, University of Leicester, 1985).
11. Davies and Crousaz, *Local Authority*.
12. Ibid. p. 18.
13. Cliffe, *Community Work*, p. 86.

7

Community Workers and Politicians

Introduction

From the late 1960s, influenced by projects like the CDP, community workers increasingly came to view their activities as political in nature. The growing trend to a more directive approach based on the more explicit expression of the workers own ideological stance inevitably made community work a more controversial activity. This was especially so when the workers were employed by the state but might be seen to be directly involved in the promotion of political action by the community which challenged the decision-making of elected members. The orientation of community workers to the needs of disadvantaged minority groups often placed them in a position where conflict with the predominant interests of the community, as represented by elected councillors, was likely. However, the degree to which the politicisation of community work was to be problematic, varied enormously as a reflection of the interactions between the relative dispositions of the workers and the political values expressed by politicians, particularly at local government level, though occasionally too at national level.

It might be anticipated that the higher the degree of congruence of political values between community workers and local politicians, the lower the likelihood of conflict. In an authority such as Strathclyde, therefore, with an explicit anti-deprivation and community development policy, a relatively low degree of conflict could be anticipated, especially given the generally non-controversial nature of the content of workers activities as described in Chapter 3.

This chapter explores the views of the Regional Council politicians held by the community work staff and reveals that there is still a degree of tension despite the apparently sympathetic environment for the practice of community work.

Contacts with Politicians and their Implications for Workers' Perceptions

Whilst it would not be anticipated that politicians will be a primary contact group, nonetheless, as has already been noted, generally, contact is limited (2.8% of work time). It is slightly higher for Seniors and Community Development Organisers than their colleagues.

The content of these contacts suggests that especially for Community Work Assistants and Community Workers, the contacts arose as a component of work with community groups more often relating to District Council than Regional Council services, particularly housing. This being so, the level of contact with the elected members of the Council actually responsible for community work was very low indeed. Only six workers attended any committee meetings of Regional or District Council; since half of these were Community Development Organisers this was the only group for whom it was a notable activity. Few workers then, directly observed politicians in their formal roles.

A significant majority (65%) of contact time with politicians was undertaken jointly with other parties to the community work process, particularly members of the community, most commonly in formal meetings of non-statutory groups. It may be reasonably presumed that such contacts were primarily focused on issues arising in the community rather than on community work practice itself. This is indicated by the content analysis of non-statutory group meetings which showed the primary focus to be provision of community premises and amenities; work with the unemployed; housing campaigns; resource work; and intermediate treatment/youth and children's work. In this context workers would observe the dispositions of councillors to different types of community need and response which would no doubt be a significant influence on the way that they perceived politicians.

Though it is not possible from the 1983 data to provide a precise picture of the interactions between the workers and politicians, it is suggested that the generally low level of contact and the degree to which the contact occurred in the context of meetings in which the primary focus was not community work itself but the problems it responds to, may mean that judgements made by workers of politicians' attitudes may have been derived from limited direct evidence.

The first question to which the workers were asked to respond was: 'What do you think Strathclyde Regional Council [that is, the elected members collectively] hope will be achieved by the employment of community workers?' This required them to take an overview of the outlook of elected members. Since very few workers appear to have observed the collective operation of councillors the views that they expressed may be presumed to have been derived from a mixture of generalisations from more specific experiences, the formal written policy statements of the Regional Council in relation to community work and deprivation, hearsay evidence from colleagues, rumour and even fantasy about how politicians may see them. The material in this Chapter may therefore say as much about the beliefs of the workers about politicians as it does about their direct experience of them. This is not altogether surprising. As Rossetti[1] has pointed out in discussing community participation in the London Borough of Southwark:

> 'internal politics in large organisations be they local government, industry, university, etc., are often associated with the personal and group fantasies of those who work in them about who really wields power and influence, about how much of it they have and about who is in league with whom.'

She goes on to say that knowledge will often 'rely on indirect experience in which, it is suggested, rumour or fantasy play a considerable part'.

The other two questions on which the material in this Chapter is based also considered elected members on a collective basis. Respondents were asked what aspects of their work during the recorded month they thought Strathclyde Regional Council would value most and least highly in relation to their hopes for achievement through employment of community workers which had been identified in response to the first question. The procedures for analysis of this data were the same as those for material in Chapters 5 and 6.

Workers' Views of the Aspirations of the Regional Councillors

Examining the general aspirations first, respondents were asked to indicate what they thought the elected members collectively would feel about community work. The respondents made just less than three distinct comments each on average.

Two categories occupied equal first place in terms of popularity. One of these challenged the legitimacy of the question in that it indicates that a substantial proportion of the sample (31.5%) found it difficult to identify the objectives of the Council. They commented that there was lack of clarity in the thinking of the Council both with regard to community development and the overall deprivation strategy. Two workers even went on to suggest that they were not convinced that all councillors 'even know that they employ community workers'! However, all of the workers identifying themselves with this comment offered other comments as well.

The uncertainty indicated by this category is also reflected in other comments discussed below. However, it is interesting that in equal first place was a category which suggested a conscious aspiration on the part of elected members that community work should lead to anti-deprivation work as set out in the Council's policy documents. It was, in fact, distinguished by direct use of phrases indicating anti-deprivation work in areas designated as APTs by the Regional Council, hence comments like 'to do something about deprivation in APTs'; 'implement the deprivation strategy'; 'solve local problems in deprived areas'.

In third place was a much more general category which emphasised the role of community workers in facilitating communication between the Council and community about needs. The emphasis appeared to be on the promotion of dialogue between community and Council with a view to collaborative responses.

The category occupying fourth place, rather than specifying goals for community work, emphasised disapproval by the Council of certain types of community work activity. A quarter of the sample indicated that they felt the Council lacked commitment to work which deals with contentious issues or adopts conflictual tactics. Typical comments were: 'there is a lack of Council commitment to community work when dealing with contentious issues'; 'adopting community action rather than community care approaches'; 'acting as a politiciser'.

In fifth equal place was a further comment which questioned the validity of perceiving the Council as a collectivity. These comments did not indicate what the Council hoped community work would achieve but argued, no doubt legitimately, that the commitment, expectations and understanding of councillors vary greatly. Though only one comment referred specifically to this producing 'mixed messages' for community workers, this was the general implication.

In equal fifth place was a category which suggests that the achievements which the Council seeks may be more cosmetic than real. This category emphasises the use of community development as a public relations tool which creates the pretence of an active response to the problems of deprivation, but is in reality an exercise to improve the image of the Council – hence, comments like 'to be seen to be doing something' or 'vote catching'.

Further comments suggested that workers believed the Council valued community care, voluntary service and self-help schemes in the community, whilst others were more vociferous and aggressive in nature. A few even suggested, not just a cosmetic exercise, but a deliberate conspiracy to direct community energy and attention from tackling what these community workers saw as 'real issues' – hence comments like 'to provide social policing', or 'to keep the natives quiet'.

As in the previous Chapters, it is useful to look at the overall balance of negative, neutral or positive comments and consider any differences between the worker groups. This evidence shows almost equal proportions of negative, neutral and positive comments suggesting a high degree of uncertainty about community workers' views of the hopes of the Council for their work. This no doubt led to a somewhat ambivalent relationship between them and their sponsors. There was little correlation between status and outlook of workers. These figures when compared with those from question 1, discussed in Chapter 5, do not suggest that the neutral and negative comments can be explained merely as the frustrations of workers with radical aspirations working in an unsympathetic environment.

Comparison of the rank ordering of comment categories in relation to the variables of age, sex, work location and qualification also produced few very obvious differences in orientation. However, it is worth noting that, in relation to work location, there appeared to be a tendency for workers not located in a social work base to be more negative than their colleagues. Noting, from the previous Chapter, the more negative outlook of workers in social work settings towards their managers, it could be that those with a greater detachment from their employing department were more likely to perceive constraints as lying in political relationships.

Workers' Evaluation of their Practice Relative to the Ascribed Aspirations of the Regional Councillors

Positive

Turning briefly to an exploration of the actual activities of the workers which they believed would be valued by the Regional Councillors, the comments had a high degree of homogeneity. They emphasised the kinds of activity which belong to an essentially conservative and consensual frame of reference for community work. They were service-orientated strategies for community change which value self-help highly, rather than strategies which make demands for change on resource and power holders who both deliver and control the quality of public services in the community. Thus the most popular comment category was community care schemes, followed by the provision of community premises and amenities which were largely seen as facilitating community care.

The third most popular category was corporate working and was a reflection of policies in relation to neighbourhood management and development. Other important categories thought to be highly valued were intermediate treatment/youth and children's work; resource work; advice and information work; information gathering and research; and work to encourage community, elected members and officials to work together. The first category potentially involving more campaigning orientations is work with tenants' associations, but even here many comments were hedged with qualifications such as 'this work takes the sting out of volatile groups'.

Exploring the evidence in terms of breakdown by age, sex, work location or qualification, it is very tentatively suggested that male and older workers may have felt that they should have been involved in more politically delicate organisational activities whilst women and younger workers noted more service orientations.

Negative

In relation to activities that it was thought would not be valued highly by the Council, there was a very widespread, though a relatively small number of comments. However, they were generally consistent with those in relation to the first half of the question.

The most popular negative category was informal discussions. This relates to the unplanned contacts in the time budget analysis and may suggest that workers did not believe councillors would see the necessity for it or that they had doubts about its value as an activity themselves. In second place was administration and clerical work. The researcher suspects that this reflected an over-estimation of the actual amount of time spent on the activity. Work on housing campaigns was in equal second place and was thought not to be valued as it implied more aggressive collective action on the part of the community groups. Other activities thought not to be valued by councillors were work with other community development staff; general work with community groups; and work with the unemployed. Some of these are difficult to interpret. The first was possibly a concern that councillors might regard the activity as unproductive or that it usurped their authority in policy making, whilst the second might indicate that workers doubted the understanding of councillors of the process of community work. In relation to the unemployed, it was more the style of work than the group on which it focuses which was of concern.

Comment

Comparison of the policy formulated by elected members (see Chapter 1) with this evidence suggests that the tendency to believe councillors hold relatively conservative views of community work would not appear to be wholly justified, though the policy documents contain some confusion. Part of the problem may be, however, that the workers did not experience the elected members collectively but as individuals operating either as local representatives or as key members of committees with an interest in the local issues under discussion. It is quite possible therefore that, as Corina has suggested,[2] community workers meet elected members in a variety of different roles which may lead them to operate in ways which are not necessarily consistent with specific policies in relation to community work. In a highly complex, multiple goal organisation, such as a Regional Council serving 2.5 million people, this is hardly surprising. What is more surprising is that, given the degree of belief that there was potential and actual tension and conflict between workers and elected members, more time was not being given to direct development of dialogue than the network analysis of Chapter 4 reveals.

In seeking explanations for the tensions which are apparent between the workers and the elected members, a possibility worthy of consideration is that it arose from the degree to which the functions of community workers and councillors overlap. Given that the predominant form of contact between the two groups appeared to occur in the context of discussions of local community problems, councillors were likely to have been operating primarily in their roles as ward representatives rather than as members of council committees which carry managerial and policy functions in relation to particular services throughout the Region or District. As Hampton suggests:[3]

'The classical liberal theory of representative democracy affirms that the M.P. or local councillor is the communicating link between the governed and the governors. The elected representative is expected not only to present the complaints of his constituents, and to remedy the injustices they suffer, but also to embrace their opinions.'

Though Hampton goes on to say that 'such a simple view has little relevance to mass democracy,' it can be argued that this perception of role is one to which many elected members appear to cling, despite the fact that rational assessment of their behaviour indicates that a vast range of influences other than those of ward residents actually inform their role playing. Most significant among these are the influences of party policy, the party caucus, membership of particular committees serving the electorate as a whole, influence of the officer system in advising councillors on options open to them, the influence of the personal ideology/values of the members, the constraints imposed by countervailing political influences and the status of the particular member within the party or committee.

The contention that elected members may see themselves in this classical representative function can be supported by reference to the Report of the Policy Review Group on Community Development Services[4] in Strathclyde. Having already identified one of the key factors affecting the disadvantaged areas of the Region as 'a sense of estrangement from councillors and M.P.s,' the document later states that 'the role of the councillor is to represent the community but he has been inadequately equipped to do this in a variety of ways'. It would not be reasonable to argue that the document fails to recognise the complexity of councillors' roles but emphasis is clearly given to their local representative function. The report states that 'it is crucially important to community development that councillors, as public representatives, are seen to matter, and an increased role at policy making level would complement the increased role at local level which we propose in our recommendations'.

The overlap between the perceptions of elected members of their role and that of community workers is demonstrable by reference to the history of community work in the UK. When the 1968 Gulbenkian Report[5] stated that 'in short, community work is a means of giving life to local democracy,' it was clearly indicating not only the political nature of community work but, in a sense too, it was indicating a concern about the apparent failures of local representative democracy.

This concern with compensation for deficiencies of the local democratic process has been a consistent theme of literature in community work in the UK over the last two decades. Thomas,[6] for example, describes community work as being concerned with a 'deliberate policy of franchisal development' which is concerned with working with community groups to promote 'political responsibility', 'political significance' and 'political competence'. His emphasis is on minority and disadvantaged groups which have become estranged from the political process and this was a central problem recognised by Strathclyde Regional Council in the development of its community work policy. Elsewhere, Thomas, writing with Henderson and Jones,[7] suggests:

'Within society, community work occupies a marginal position in relation to major political economic and social welfare institutions and forces. Community workers tend, on the whole, to work with marginal groups, particularly those left with little in the way of resources, status, power and ambition... Community workers may be seen as people who help others to cross boundaries that they themselves invariably remain outside of. This interjacent location of community work is implicitly conveyed in some of the more common role descriptions such as mediator, broker, advocate, facilitator and interpreter.'

These roles are a familiar concern in the training of community workers and can be regarded as generally acknowledged features of community work. For example, in discussing the skills required of community workers, the Central Council for Education and Training in Social Work curriculum study[8] on the teaching of community work refers to the importance of 'political skills' and states:

'Skill in coping with the tensions and crises that arise in the process of intervention negotiation and advocacy and in the identification of issues involving the use and distribution of power will be required in a variety of situations in formal organisations, in informal meetings with colleagues or with local residents in the neighbourhood.'

Given the overlap between the roles of community workers in stimulating democratic participation or more direct forms of campaigning by minority interests, and the local representative functions of elected members, it is not surprising that there is some degree of tension. In his review of community work in the Social Work Department of the Regional Council,[9] the Director of Social Work sought to clarify the relationship in order to minimise tensions. He said:

'The roles of community workers and local members are mutually supportive ... The community worker in assisting the community to identify its needs and interests is in a position to contribute to the effectiveness of the formal political representation of political interests exercised by the local member. Conversely, the community worker, as an agent of the Council's social strategy, can look to members to support initiatives taken in line with this objective ... The potential exists, however, for misunderstanding.'

Though acknowledging the potential tensions, the report appears to attempt to curtail the functions of community workers when it states that 'the community worker's role is never that of representing or speaking on the behalf of the community'.[10]

Such a limitation, whilst it may be an understandable attempt to differentiate the functions of elected representatives from those of community workers, is not consistent with roles that have been prescribed for them in much community work literature. This is not to argue that representative roles have been regarded as the central function of community work but to acknowledge that they are an accepted part of the repertoire of the community worker. Butcher et al,[11] for example, discuss the role of community workers under the headings of 'enabler', 'broker', 'advocate' and 'activist', whilst Henderson and Thomas,[12] talking about transactions between community groups and other systems, refer to the worker roles of 'delegate' and 'plenipotentiary'. Given that such terms clearly indicate that workers would expect to carry representative roles to some degree, tension with the formal political system is likely to be endemic.

The ambivalence revealed in the comments of the Strathclyde workers with regard to elected members illustrates the complexity of the relationship. In particular, it suggests that community workers may see themselves sometimes as the collaborative allies of elected members, at others as in direct conflict with them about the definition of, and appropriate responses to, local needs. It is suggested, however, that the limited degree of direct contact between them may imply that the way workers see the relationship is not always informed by a direct knowledge of the actual dispositions of councillors towards them. Further, the general lack of evidence of extensive and analytical work by these community workers about community problems and the dynamics at work in promoting them and inhibiting change (see Chapter 3), also suggests that attitudes may be derived from generalisations about councillor behaviour rather than accurate information. Since community workers in local authority employment are ultimately accountable to elected members, it is in their interests to attempt to negotiate the relationship with more clarity than the evidence of this study appears to suggest.

The importance of the promotion of the relationship with politicians has been emphasised by Young[13] who, as an elected member centrally involved in the promotion of community work and anti-deprivation policy in Strathclyde, has said:

'many community workers have fallen into the familiar trap of assuming that people called politicians possess political skills. At the local level the only skills which the experience of local government develops well are those of survival – not of social change.'

He goes on to argue that community workers need to work with politicians to develop strategic and organisational skills suggesting that 'many community workers are indeed self indulgent in choosing to work with community groups ... rather than the more challenging environment of politics and other professions'.

How extensively other politicians would acknowledge such deficiencies may be one of the dilemmas which inhibits community workers in their engagement with elected members, but the area deserves more attention. Undertaken without the necessary skills and insight the process may however become counter-productive in that it may simply promote political action in relation to sectional interests, and damage the capacity of local government to act equitably between different local interests. As Corina[14] has said:

'what might be counter productive is the type of politicisation which triggers off sectional pressures, compelling a response from an authority which actually reduces the chances of meeting the needs of the most deprived. What is not needed, in other words, is pressure which reverses the efforts to effect redistributive measures.'

Given the essentially local neighbourhood orientation of the Strathclyde workers, their lack of systematic analysis of community need and their view of the parochialism of the community groups, this is potentially a very real problem.

To facilitate more effective relationships with the elected members it is necessary for community workers to develop a relatively sophisticated understanding of the complexity of of politicians' roles and their relationships with the local government officer system. In an authority such as Strathclyde, where relationships between the community and both officers and politicians are often mediated through participation structures, this is particularly important. It is important to consider carefully the need to sustain relationships with elected members which engage them in the concerns of the community organisation before thy arise in crucial forums for decision making. In other words, it may be necessary, to a degree, to pander to the prevailing belief of many elected members in a representative democratic process and to engage them as early as possible in a dialogue about controversial community proposals. Such proposals are much more likely to be carefully considered and supported if they emanate from organisations in the community which have established their credibility as having a history of serving community interests and being able to demonstrate popular support. As Darke and Walker[15] have suggested in reviewing councillors' attitudes to participation procedures in South Yorkshire:

> 'councillors are extremely concerned about legitimate representation. Opinions backed by substantial and politically acceptable support have greater authority and political impact. If views are presented in an acceptable package of moderation which encloses constructive proposals, the principle of representative democracy is not threatened. However, the disruptive or radical proposal may also carry further implied threats, namely to operating ideologies and principles as well as to the oiled and established procedures of local government and administration.'

Notes

1.   F. Rossetti, 'Politics and Participation: A Case Study' in P. Curno (ed.) *Political Issues and Community Work* (London: Routledge and Kegan Paul, 1978) p. 156.

2.   L. Corina, 'Local Government Decision Making – Some Influences on Elected Members' Role Playing', *Papers in Community Studies*, No. 2. (Department of Social Administration and Social Work, University of York, 1975).

3.   W. Hampton, *Democracy and Community – a Study of Politics in Sheffield* (London: Oxford University Press, 1970) p. 214.

4.   A. Worthington, *Policy Review Group on Community Development Services* ('the Worthington Report') (Strathclyde Regional Council, 1978) p. 34.

5.   The Gulbenkian Foundation, *Community Work and Social Change* (London: Longman, 1968) p. 5.

6.   D.N. Thomas, *The Making of Community Work* (London: George Allen and Unwin, 1983) pp. 71, 73.

7.   P. Henderson, D. Jones and D.N. Thomas, *The Boundaries of Change in Community Work* (London: George Allen and Unwin, 1980) p. 3.

8. Central Council for Education and Training in Social Work, *Social Work Curriculum Study – The Teaching of Community Work* (1974) p. 20.

9. Director of Social Work, *Helping the Community to Organise* (Strathclyde Regional Council, 1984) para. 4.6.

10. Ibid.

11. H. Butcher, P. Collis, A. Glen and P. Sills, *Community Groups in Action – Case Studies and Analysis* (London: Routledge and Kegan Paul, 1980) p. 254.

12. P. Henderson and D.N. Thomas, *Skills in Neighbourhood Work* (Allen and Unwin, 1980) p. 104.

13. R. Young, 'Community Development – its Political and Administrative challenge', *Social Work Today* (February 1977) reprinted in P. Henderson and D.N. Thomas, *Readings in Community Work* (London: George Allen and Unwin, 1981) p. 163.

14. Corina, 'Local Government', p. 28.

15. R. Darke and R. Walker, *Local Government and the Public* (London: Leonard Hill, 1977) p. 85.

8

Community Workers and Community Groups

Introduction

In a completely non-directive approach to community work the commitment of workers to the will of the groups with whom they work would be absolute. It is doubtful, however, if such an approach has ever been adopted, for workers have always reserved the right to dissociate themselves from ethically unacceptable activities. It is certainly the case though that community workers have become increasingly inclined to place greater emphasis on their own values and ideologies in deciding with whom they will work and in what way. (Indeed when asked to rate this factor alongside others which might be influential they regarded it as third most important of 14 factors.) This shift varies greatly between individual workers and is in all cases tempered by the influence of the nature of needs in the area and the dispositions of the consumers and the sponsors of community work practice. Just as community workers have the sanction of withdrawal of support from community groups whose activities are not acceptable to them, so, equally, do community groups have the option of rejection of the worker, or sponsors, the withdrawal of funding or other organisational measures to curb activities. Community work practice, then, involves a complex set of boundary negotiations between the three parties to the process which critically influence what will actually be set as practice goals. These goals are obviously also crucially affected by the motivation, capacity, opportunity and resources available to tackle the targets for change, whilst also being influenced by the assessment of the capacity of the targets to resist change.

In approaching the material in this Chapter it is important to be aware of the complexity of the process of determining what community work will actually take place. In the previous three Chapters insight has been gained into the aspirations of the workers for their own practice. It is apparent that the sample examined in this research held a variety of ideological and value dispositions towards their work. Similarly it will be apparent that their assessments of the aspirations of their managers and the Regional Council for their work indicates that many workers believed there to be inherent tensions between themselves and their sponsors. In this Chapter we examine their view of the aspirations of the community groups with whom they worked and their beliefs as to the value which the groups placed on the work that they undertook during the recorded month. Comparison of these findings with the previous material provides a basis for understanding the workers' perceptions of the overall interactions which largely determine what they do.

Workers were asked: 'what do you think the members of the community groups with whom you work hope your community work will achieve?' They were then asked what aspects of their actual work during the recorded month they thought the community groups with whom they worked would value most and least highly, relative to their ascribed aspirations identified in the first question.

The procedures for the analysis of the material were the same as those for Chapters 5 to 7.

Before examining the evidence in relation to the way that the workers perceive the interests of the community groups with whom they work, it is worth reminding ourselves of the level and kind of contact that each group of workers had with community groups (see Chapter 4). Significantly higher proportions of work time were spent with members of the community (mostly community group members) by Community Work Assistants and Community Workers (38.8% and 35.2% respectively) than by Community Development Organisers and Seniors (11.9% and 16.9% respectively). The first two groups have a more consistent development role with particular groups and were therefore much more likely to feel a sense of loyalty, or possibly even accountability, to the interests of the organisations of the community.

Workers' Views of the Aspirations of Community Groups

Exploring the general aspirations first, the workers were asked to indicate what they thought the community groups with whom they worked hoped community work would achieve. The question provoked the highest absolute number of comments, and it was also the one which produced the most consistent pattern of response.

Examining the rank order of categories of comment, one was outstanding, made by no less than 83.1% of the sample. The category simply indicates that what community groups want to achieve through the activities they undertake with the community worker is a resolution to the particular problems which have brought them into being. It might be argued that such a statement is self-evident but the nature of the problems specified in these answers indicates a very interesting feature of community groups concerns in that the issues which were described appeared to indicate self-interested and essentially parochial concerns. This is not to be deprecated as, given the kinds of problems faced in the disadvantaged areas of the Region, such concerns are of great importance and undoubted legitimacy. Nonetheless it is interesting to contrast more limited aspirations believed to be held by members of community groups with the broader aspirations which workers indicated they held for the community groups, as revealed by the responses to question 1, discussed in Chapter 5.

The second most common category was a slightly indirect answer to the question in that, rather than defining the achievements which are hoped for, respondents commented instead on the role that members of groups expected workers to perform. The roles specified ranged from passive to highly active and were of interest in revealing the kind of expectations which workers believed their consumer groups to have of them. Roles identified were 'enabler'; 'supporter'; 'ally'; 'organiser'; 'resource provider'; 'stirrer'; 'advocate'; '(super) fixer'; and 'clerical service provider'.

In third place, workers commented on the difficulty of providing a generalised answer to the question when the hopes of groups change over time with changing experiences, levels of worker contact and so on.

The fourth category expressed the confidence of some workers in the independence of community groups, though whether such a hope would be consistent with the roles such as fixer, resource provider, advocate or organiser, as identified in the second ranked category, is questionable. Comments here referred to the members of community groups hoping that they would 'come to stand on their own feet'; 'do things for themselves'; or 'resist takeover by the community worker'.

The aspirations of groups to obtain direct financial aid was fifth in rank order. Typical of comments here was 'the members of community groups hope they will receive financial aid to develop services'. The most common sources of finance specified were Urban Aid and section 12, *Social Work (Scotland) Act* 1968 grants.

The top five categories accounted for the substantial majority of the comments made. Other not infrequent comments referred to 'hopes for a higher level of community participation'; 'a more sensitive response from local government'; 'the development of individual as well as group capacities to tackle problems'; and the hope that 'the community will develop a wider perspective on issues and problems not exclusive to their own community'. The emphasis of the remaining comments, however, was either on the quality of the relationship between the group and the community it sought to represent or the group and the resource holder it sought to influence.

As a whole, the responses to the question appear to indicate that the workers' viewed the community groups as having generally limited and localised aspirations for change. They also appeared to take a conservative view of the aspirations of the groups.

The homogeneity of response in general was also reflected in the lack of any major variation between the sample strata or in relation to age, sex, work location or professional qualification.

Overall, the view adopted by the workers of community group aspirations was more conservative than their own (see Chapter 5) but suggested a consistency with the actual activities they undertook as discussed in Chapter 3.

Workers' Evaluation of their Practice Relative to the Ascribed Aspirations of the Community Groups

Positive Aspects

The aspects of their work that the workers believed the community would most value reflected their view of community groups being parochial in orientation. Most popular categories were resource work; advice and information work (the majority of comments specifying that this is to groups not individuals); general work with community groups; and provision of community premises facilities and amenities. All four of the leading categories bore close relation to one another in their emphasis on supporting the process of community group activity.

Other quite commonly cited categories were work with housing campaigns; IT, youth and children's work; media work; work with individuals and families; and work to directly influence Regional and District Council Departments.

The general pattern held across the sample as a whole though the more extensive interest in housing campaigns expressed by Community Workers and social work-located staff is worthy of note.

Negative Aspects

Turning to those aspects of their work which workers felt community groups would least value, the general characteristic seemed to be any activity which took workers away from a direct relationship with the groups. Thus, work with other community development staff; lack of availability; time not spent in the area; work with other groups; written work, recording and report preparation; administration and clerical work; and training, were all commonly cited categories.

In relation to non-valued activities there was more variation than elsewhere in the result, between sub-groups of workers. The frustration expressed by women about activities which took them away from direct involvement in the activities of particular groups was especially noteworthy. CQSW qualified staff expressed the same concerns. The overall impression from this evidence is that workers believed the groups to feel negatively about their professional, collaborative and development activities which operated independently of the groups. Workers portrayed a rather self-centred view of the groups. It suggests that workers had not established an understanding of the breadth of roles they were expected to perform or of the nature of their accountability and loyalties. However, the loyalty of workers to the community groups did not appear to be particularly problematic, for the aspirations of the groups, as indicated here, were consistent with Social Work Department policy for community work and with the kinds of activity which community workers generally undertook.

Comparison with the 1989 Audit

Though by 1989 there was evidence of increasing levels of campaigning work and some growth in inter-neighbourhood organisation especially in relation to housing issues, the overall pattern of work was very similar. The primary attention remained with local concerns and this suggests that there has been little change in the nature of relationships between workers and groups. In the absence of directly comparable evidence this is a speculative conclusion.

Comment

Elsewhere, in applying the community problem solving model developed by Spergel,[1] I[2] have argued that community workers carry three basic functions in relating to community groups: organisational; inter-organisational; and intra-organisational. The first is concerned with the process of creating organisational structure within a community by which it can undertake evaluation and diagnosis of its situation and hence prescribe for its own needs. The inter-organisational level is concerned with the relationship between organised communities and the institutions and agencies which control the means by which such groups can obtain redress of grievances. The intra-organisational level is concerned with the conflicts which are internal to a community and its representative organisations and inhibit its ability to develop a coherent organised resolution of its needs.

Using this formulation, it can be argued that in situations where there is currently no (or no effective) organised response to community problems, the primary task of the worker is to help the community to find mechanisms by which it can address its collective needs. Usually this involves drawing together a group of activists from the community of interest (itself commonly neighbourhood based), assisting it to clarify the nature of the problem and possible resolutions, identify tactics and strategy, and support the organisation in implementing these. This sounds quite straightforward but, as the literature on the practice of community work consistently makes clear, it is a highly complex process, largely because disadvantaged people are likely to have very low expectations of the potential for change and need considerable support to achieve effectiveness. This is not a statement about innate abilities but a realistic recognition of the pressures experienced in daily life which not only sap energy but undermine belief in the potential for change. It is these factors which lead Twelvetrees,[3] for example, when discussing the time scales of community worker involvement to say: 'but as far as deprived, poor or oppressed communities are concerned the process is very long indeed and the effect of community work intervention should be measured in terms of decades rather than years.'

It is these same factors which not only affect time scale but also lead to stress on the intra-organisational processes of work with community groups. These processes concern the maintenance of group cohesion and direction, sustaining members through internal conflicts and frustrations in their relations with outsiders whose support they require or whose attitudes or decisions need change. As I have suggested: 'in many respects it is the skill of the community worker in this role which is most important in determining the success of the community work process, yet it is the role that is least visible to outsiders.'[4]

Henderson and Thomas[5] stress the need for community workers to be supportive towards community groups. They say:

'The group particularly needs the support and encouragement of the worker at times when its energies and enthusiasms are low, and it feels it has suffered setbacks, or achieved little, in reaching its goals. The worker can often be supportive in and commitment that seem to be waning in group members...'

This brief reminder of the character of the relationship between workers and groups in neighbourhood-based community work in disadvantaged areas is provided because it illustrates issues likely to be prevalent for community workers in the sample. It may also help to explain some of their perceptions of the activities which groups with which they work valued.

As Runciman[6] has argued, there appears to be a correlation between the level of disadvantage which people experience and their belief in and horizons for change. Thus these workers, operating in multiply-disadvantaged communities, may be accurately reflecting the aspirations of the groups with which they work when they stress concern with more immediate and parochial matters.

Just as significantly, however, it is argued that the difficulties outlined above, which are apparent to practitioners in supporting effective community group action, will tend to generate a high degree of identification of workers with the interests of the groups. Workers whose actions may well have been catalytic in the promotion of an organised response from the community inevitably feel both a strong sense of responsibility for, and loyalty to, the process of community development. Butcher et al[7] in a detailed study of the functioning of five community groups comment:

'The level of a community worker's involvement in a group is likely to be greater when he has been involved in establishing it, and when group members have easy access to his office or the immediate area of his activity.'

This latter point is also significant for the sample studied here, particularly the Community Work Assistants and Community Workers who spent a very high proportion of their work time in direct contact with members of the community, particularly a relatively small number of active community group members.

It is not difficult in the light of these points to see why the tenor of comments in this chapter focuses on the meeting of locally-defined needs and the adequate resourcing of community groups to achieve their ends. The evidence of Chapter 3, on the work that the sample actually undertook, indicates that a high proportion of their activities did focus on the meeting of the kinds of needs which they believed community groups to have. This may not be entirely consistent with their own aspirations (as identified in Chapter 5) which suggests that the community groups, as consumers of the services of community work staff, exert a pivotal influence on what community workers actually do. Fortunately, this produces consistency with the expectations of the Director of Social Work when he states that 'the basic distinguishing feature of community work is that its primary focus within the process of community development is on assisting communities to organise around locally defined needs and issues'.[8]

If it were not consistent, it is suggested that the negative attitudes to social work management expressed in Chapter 6, would be likely to have precipitated a much higher degree of overt conflict than was actually apparent. The workers appeared to accept a more limited set of objectives than was indicated by their own aspirations as discussed in Chapter 5, largely out of a loyalty to, or identification with, their consumers rather than out of acknowledgement of the appropriateness of the policy. I pointed out at the beginning of the chapter and as Butcher et al[9] put it:

> 'Community workers are not autonomous in defining their role with community groups. The interplay between a community group, the employing agency and a worker's own attitudes determines the range and nature of the roles he performs.'

In the case of this group of workers it appears that the potential for conflict between these interests was tempered by the critical influence of the community groups which appeared to define the parameters of community work practice in a way which left little need for dispute about the kinds of activities with which workers became involved. Conflict may therefore often be as concerned with the postures that the various parties to the community work process adopt as it is with the realities of what workers do.

Notes

1. I.A. Spergel, *Community Problem Solving – the Delinquency Example* (University of Chicago Press, 1969).
2. A. Barr, 'The Practice of Neighbourhood Community Work', *Papers in Community Studies*, No. 12 (University of York, 1977).
3. A. Twelvetrees, *Community Work* (London: Macmillan, 1982) p. 65.
4. Barr, 'Practice' p. 21.
5. P. Henderson and D.N. Thomas, *Skills in Neighbourhood Work* (London: George Allen and Unwin, 1980) p. 212.
6. W.G. Runciman, *Relative Deprivation and Social Justice* (London: Routledge and Kegan Paul, 1966).
7. H. Butcher, P. Collis, A. Glen and P. Sills, *Community Groups in Action – Case Studies and Analysis* (London: Routledge and Kegan Paul, 1980) p. 255.

8. Director of Social Work, *Helping the Community to Organise* (Strathclyde Regional Council, 1984) para. 3.4.
9. Butcher et al, *Community Groups*, p. 254.

Part IV
Reflections

9

Community Work and Local Government

In these final Chapters, important themes related to the experience of community work in Strathclyde will be explored.

Being a study of community work sponsored by a major local authority, the tensions between the objectives and characteristics of the local state as a community work employer, the aspirations of the community workers themselves and the nature of community work are of particular interest. It is important to review recent trends in local government pertinent to community work practice, and to place the findings in the context of debate within British community work literature about community workers' relationships with the state. This is the subject-matter of the next two Chapters.

Recent Trends in Local Government

Community work is one of the more recent occupations to emerge in local government, though it is by no means universal. Equally, its own ambivalence about whether it wants to be professionalised sets it apart from most other occupational groups. Nonetheless, it has emerged in the last 20 years as an apparently established feature of the activities of some local authorities like Strathclyde. Publications such as the AMA Report *Community Development – The Local Authority Role*[1] also indicate an increasing interest in its wider application.

In discussing community work in the local state it is important to set its development in the context of trends in local government. Boaden[2] has argued that there are two powerful forces critical to local government – the need to be 'democratic' and the need to be 'efficient'. Though it is not always clear what is meant by these terms they are generally viewed as being in tension with one another. He argues:

'At the centre of the conflict between the two criteria of democracy and efficiency in local government lies the important question of the most appropriate scale of operation and organisation of local government. For those who believe in participant democracy, "small is beautiful" while for those who want efficient local government "big is better"!'

He suggests that the growth in scale of local government in this century reflects a desire for efficiency in an increasingly complex urban industrial society. It gives rise to four major themes which he identifies as 'functional fragmentation'; 'centralisation of government'; 'professionalisation of service provision'; and 'the increasing remoteness of government from people'.[3]

These themes are all relevant to consideration of the roles and dilemmas of community work and the local state.

Functional Fragmentation
In relation to functional fragmentation, the increasing complexity and range of the statutory obligations of local government has seen a steady increase in the number of departments and the range of specialised workers within them. To some extent this trend has been checked in the last few years with restrictions on local government expenditure; nonetheless, the local authority remains a highly complex bureaucratic structure with consequent difficulties in relating to its consumers in straightforward and understandable ways. At least one of the attractions in employing community workers is that they will act as intermediaries between citizens and the council. The Strathclyde Regional Review of Community Work in 1978,[4] for example, refers to the 'community worker who is expected to carry out a *pivotal* role between community and authority' (their emphasis). It is worth noting too that this function was acknowledged by the workers in this study as a central aspiration of elected members for their work (see Chapter 7). In discussing the workers' views of the community groups they also referred extensively to being expected to be a channel for communication between communities and the local authority, particularly in terms of obtaining resources for local activities (see Chapter 8). In that the actual activities of the workers (see Chapter 3) placed

heavy emphasis on the servicing of the needs of community groups by assisting them to obtain resources of various kinds, this intermediary function can be seen to be extensive. It is noticeable, however, that in discussing their own aspirations for their work (see Chapter 5) the workers did not give it high priority. In his 1984 review[5] of community work though, the Director of Social Work acknowledged the centrality of the role but stressed that the function of the community worker is not to speak either for the community or for the Council. He says:

> 'The worker's primary concern is to assist the community to maintain a dialogue with the authority at a level and in a form appropriate to the issues in question. In this sense the community worker is not a "mediator" bringing sides together, but more of a "consultant" and an enabler to the community.'

It can be argued then that the fragmentation of functions and increased complexity in local government is in a sense being compensated for by the employment of community workers and developments such as area liaison committees. This is not unique in the public sector: for example, the emergence of Community Health Councils in relation to the National Health Service, some of which adopt a community development approach, represents a similar trend.

Since, despite current trends towards privatisation, it is difficult not to envisage a continuation of the complex functional fragmentation of local government, it seems likely that this may secure a long-term role for community work as an antidote. However, the way in which community work is used, and indeed whether it is regarded as an appropriate means, will vary from authority to authority. Generally it appears to be democratic socialist authorities like Strathclyde or Sheffield which have been most attracted to this approach and it is suggested that this reflects a view that disadvantaged communities need to be empowered to ensure that positive discrimination is achieved. Without this kind of objective, more conventional public relations methods are more likely to be employed to improve public knowledge of local government services. Nor is it the case that left-wing authorities have universally promoted community work; indeed, it may be argued that in Militant-led Liverpool, for example, a centralist authoritarianism ran counter to the notion of empowerment of local community interests (illustrated, for example, in the long-running dispute between black community organisations and the council over the appointment of the community relations officer).

The form which community work in local government is likely to take must be considered carefully in terms of the particular dispositions and objectives of different employers. The potential seems to exist for radical alliances between community workers and the local state on the basis of common social ideals, but reflective evaluation of performance will be needed to measure whether outcomes are matching objectives. Community work itself is not an inherently radical occupation, as is indicated by the evidence of this study, and the objectives of employers are rarely consistent or constant as power and influence in the political system shift. In particular it has to be recognised that local government does not operate independently of the influence of central government. This point leads into a discussion of the second major theme identified by Boaden, 'centralisation of government'.

Centralisation
Centralisation of power has been an inexorable trend in the post-war period. The emergence of the post-Beveridge welfare state has been a major source of the growth of local government but the statutory framework within which functions like education, personal social services or housing has developed has ensured only limited variations in forms of service provided. The welfare state itself, for example in development of income maintenance services, can be viewed as a major feature of centralism in government. However, it is only one feature of this trend. Under socialist governments, the process of nationalisation of major industries and the idea of a planned economy were basic features of this centralism. The emergence of the radical conservatism of the present government has seen a return to free market economic principles, privatisation and enhanced roles for consumers, for example in the governance of schools, but while these aspects of state control may have been reversed for ideological reasons, other aspects of government policy, especially in relation to local government, show even greater desire for centralisation of power. Most particularly, the control of local government finance through rate capping of 'overspending' authorities and legislation to replace local rates with the community charge are central. It should not be suggested,

however, that this trend is just a consequence of the present government. Darke and Walker,[6] for example, writing in 1977 argued that 'dependent upon central finance and subject to a blanket of expenditure controls the ability of local government to respond to local needs and to innovate is increasingly hamstrung by the lack of control over necessary resources'. It would not, however, be appropriate to view local authorities as innocent victims of the process of centralisation for they have themselves shown an increasing tendency to centralisation of power, especially in councils consistently dominated by one political party. In particular, the authority of the party caucus relative to the formal committees and the council itself and the growth of corporate management have tended to place power in fewer and more remote hands. Similarly, the growth of the local authority associations, as bargaining organisations with central government, has contributed significantly to the remoteness and delocalisation of politics.

There are many more ways in which these centralising trends could be illustrated; however, the pattern is clear. What then is the connection between the process of centralisation and the role of community work, and what implications does it have for the scope of local authority-based community work practice? In relation to the first question, community work can be viewed as part of a wider reaction to centralisation based on a number of different arguments. First, that democratic principle requires citizen participation as a means of legitimising the authority of government. Secondly, that many problems have specifically local dimensions and require a response in the context of local conditions. Thirdly, that empirical principles demand that lessons are learned from direct local community experience of problems. Fourthly, that if community participation is to be realised it has to be based around concerns with which ordinary people can identify. These are often matters related to local circumstances or local manifestations of wider problems, to which people can relate more easily . Fifthly, that centralised government cannot make proper use of the valuable resources of local communities and their organisations. Sixthly, that remote centralised services tend to engender high levels of dependence and inhibit the development of local resources and self-help activity. It is not only that resources may be wasted but that local responses may be more valued and more effective because of the effort and investment people put into them. This point is

particularly reflected in ideas of partnership between public
service agencies and community and voluntary organisations
which lie, for example, behind the emergence of community
social work.

Amongst the writers who have offered a philosophical under-
pinning for the principles of localisation is Schon[7] who has
argued that:

> 'Government cannot play the role of "experimenter to the
> nation" seeking first to identify the correct solution, then to
> train society at large in its adaptation. The opportunity for
> learning is primarily in discovered systems at the periphery,
> not in the nexus of official policies at the centre.'

The principles of localisation appear from the evidence of the
study to be well established among community work staff in
Strathclyde Region Social Work Department. They were shown
to be primarily motivated by a desire to respond to conditions
and experiences in local communities, they most commonly
identified with models of community work practice which stress
the empowerment of local people in relation to their own affairs
(see Chapter 5), and the ways in which they spent their time
were consistent with this (see Chapters 2 and 3). Their practice
was in turn broadly consistent with the employer's objective[8]
that they should 'assist communities to organise around locally-
defined needs and issues'.

Concern about the persistence of centralising trends in both
central and local government and its adverse effect on local
democracy, may be central to explaining the attraction of community work to some local authorities.

Professionalisation

The theme of professionalisation of service provision was the
third identified by Boaden. Post-war growth in the scale and
responsibilities of local government has spawned a wide range
of categories of worker keen to promote their professional
status. Social workers, town planners, public health inspectors,
educational psychologists, housing officers and many others
have asserted that the knowledge, skills and responsibilities
associated with their tasks require recognition of exclusive
expertise and hence the confirming of professional status and
authority.

There has been considerable tension within community work as to whether it should seek equivalent professional status to other local government employees. Much of the difficulty has been associated with the political nature of community work objectives. Professionalisation has been viewed as casting community work primarily in service development, rather than community or social action roles. Equally, it has been argued that professional status is associated with exclusiveness on the part of an occupational group based on academic and professional qualification but that such a position contradicts basic principles of community work. These principles are concerned with empowering disadvantaged people whose influence is diminished, at least in part, precisely because they lack the status of professionals. Yet at the same time community workers express a desire, as in the sample studied here, to influence colleagues within their own and other local authority departments and recognise that one of their difficulties in so doing is that they have not been able to secure parallel professional authority.

The broader questions of professionalisation in local government have wider implications in relation to the final theme identified by Boaden, 'the increasing remoteness of government from people'. It is apparent from the experience of Strathclyde that this has much to do with the quality of relationships between local people and officers of the local authority.

Remoteness

One of the consequences of the professionalisation of local government has been a tendency to increase the authority of officers relative to elected members. Political decisions appear to have been increasingly conditioned by the administrative decisions and priorities of officers. This factor has been widely noted in discussions of local government; Cheetham et al,[9] for example, argue:

'Another feature of local government... which is not always fully appreciated, has been the development during the past century of a highly professional core of administrators to whom the politicians delegate most or all of their decision making responsibilities. Consequently the style of government in many British local authorities can be described as "administrative politics", in which most of the controversy over decision making takes place in a purely private context.'

The influence of administrators over politicians has been a concern in Strathclyde Region and, in adopting approaches such as member/officer groups to review key policy areas and in area development teams, the Council has sought to redress the balance and assert political control. Nonetheless, the influence of the professional values of officers and their power to manipulate decision making has to be acknowledged. Levin,[10] for example, has identified a series of strategies which administrators may use to ensure that their priorities are reflected in policy. He refers to 'administrative investment' where scarce administrative resources are tied up in a project before it comes to formal committee decisions by politicians. A variant on this he calls 'multiple clearance' in which the administrator gains approval for the proposal from as many sources as possible before it becomes public. Open debate is prejudiced by preconditioning participants with arguments which favour a particular outcome. Levin also refers to the 'single proposal procedure' in which debate is focused on just one of a possible range of options for tackling a problem. Evidence about the feasibility of alternative approaches is not brought forward and hence not considered. He links this to the use of the "limited study", that is, one which purports to have considered the options but is in fact biased towards a particular response. Other strategies which administrators may use include setting short deadlines for decisions, deliberately not publicising contentious matters, or "hiding" unpalatable decisions within more acceptable ones.

The adoption of strategies such as those outlined is often a reflection of the desire of the professional administrators to promote policies which are broadly congruent with their professional values and their desire to sustain continuity of policy development despite political change. The extent to which such subversive strategies are employed is open to debate and the process may not be as conscious as Levin appears to suggest. Nonetheless, it is important to recognise the contribution which they may make to the remoteness of local government.

Workers in this study have shown concerns about the influence of professional dispositions on the adherence to the social strategy. Here community workers are on delicate ground for they are formally accountable to their employing department. They may feel though that its behaviour and that of other professionals sometimes fails to reflect the principles of Council policy. In working with local community organisations and local elected members, it can be argued that community workers have an opportunity to assist in the opening up of decision making in ways which challenge the remoteness of local government.

Such a role presents some problems. In particular, it places community workers in a relationship with professional colleagues in local government in which it may be difficult to forge trust. Questions of loyalty may often be in doubt when consumer empowerment is an express objective of practice.[11]

It is not only issues of professionalisation which relate to the remoteness of local government – so too do those of fragmentation and centralisation. These too contribute to the complexity and physical remoteness of centres of government. The sheer size of local government units as they were reorganised in the 1970s and the emergence of corporate management approaches have been crucial. This is especially so in Scotland where the Regional Councils not only serve wide geographical areas and in some cases very large populations but were also given responsibility for the key services of education and social work which (apart from the case of the Inner London Education Authority until its abolition) in English conurbations remained in the lower tier. This remoteness can relate to a feeling of distance, and in multiply-disadvantaged areas, where evidence of governmental failure is all too apparent, of alienation.

Concluding Comment

It is not known whether it is a reflection of the Region's social strategy, sheer good luck, the relatively small black population around which white racism could focus or other factors, but Strathclyde has experienced little of the communal violence which hase exploded in many other British inner cities. There is undoubtedlt frustration, disillusion and anger associated with lack of jobs, poor housing and inadequate amenities, but, as the Scottish vote in the 1987 general election suggests, the blame appears to be placed squarely with central government. The Regional Social Strategy and the parallel policies of some of the District Councils, most notably in Glasgow, have identified local government with the interests of the most disadvantaged. They have not claimed that their policies alone could reverse the structural processes which lie behind the problems of disadvantage but there is more than a theoretical commitment on the part of the Regional Council to positive discrimination.

Community workers have been central to the strategy. Whilst they have expressed many frustrations about the performance of their role and commitment of their employers to the objectives set, they have been party to one of the most substantial attempts in British loval government history to build links between disadvantaged communities and the council. This has attempted to tackle the remoteness of local government and make it relevant to local needs.

Relevance has been acheived, through the targeting of Urban Programme and redirecting mainstream service priorities towards the geographical areas most characterised by multiple deprivation and establishing in them mechanisms for consulting local opinion. The use of corporate member-officer groups known as area development teams to tackle specific local issues in areas of deprivation, and the subsequent establishment of area liaison committees,the establishment of a decentralised system of small grants committees and an increasing trend to localise the premises from which departments operate, have also been significant. Criticism of the effectiveness of these approaches has been reflected in the comments of the workers studied here (see Chapters 6 and 7 particularly) and the Regional Council itself has acknowledged limitations in its approach. For example its *Social Strategy for the Eighties* states that 'we have probably expected too much of local initiatives and certainly have not provided enough support for them'.[12]

The workers studied here have, then, been operating within a local government setting which has been subject to all of the general trends which Boaden identifies. The influences of 'functional fragmentation', 'centralisation of power', 'professionalisation' and 'remoteness' from consumers are central to establishing an appreciation of the context of community work practice in local authorities not only for workers but equally for their employers and consumers.

Notes

1.   Association of Metropolitan Authorities, *Community Development – the Local Authority Role* (1989).
2.   N. Boaden, M. Goldsmith, W. Hampton and P. Stringer, *Public Participation in Local Services* (London: Longman, 1982) pp. 2, 4.
3.   Ibid. p. 5.

4.   A. Worthington, *Policy Review Group on Community Development Services* ('the Worthington Report') (Strathclyde Regional Council, 1978) p. 13.

5.   Director of Social Work, *Helping the Community to Organise* (Strathclyde Regional Council, 1984) para. 4.5.

6.   R. Darke and R. Walker, *Local Government and the Public* (London: Leonard Hill, 1977) p. 12.

7.   D. Schon, *Beyond the Stable State* (Harmondsworth: Pelican, 1973) p. 165.

8.   Director of Social Work, *Helping the Community*, para. 3.4.

9.   J. Cheetham and M.J. Hill, 'Community Work: Social Realities And Ethical Dilemmas', *British Journal of Social Work*, vol. 3, no. 3 (1973) reprinted in P. Henderson and D.N. Thomas, *Readings in Community Work* (London: George Allen and Unwin, 1981) p. 169.

10.   P. Levin, 'Opening up the Planning Process' in S. Hatch, 'Towards Participation in Social Services', *Fabian Tract*, no. 419 (1973) reprinted in Henderson and Thomas, *Readings*, pp. 109–111.

11.   See *Community Development Journal* ('Consumer Action and Community Development') (Autumn 1989).

12.   Strathclyde Regional Council, *Social Strategy for the Eighties* (1984) p. 34.

10

Community Work and the State

Though his comments have to some extent been overtaken by the emergence of Thatcherite, new right, radical conservatism, Lambert[1] has offered a useful review of a range of attitudes in community work towards the state. He provides a valuable starting point for a brief review of debate on this issue in recent community work literature.

> 'For the Conservative and the Liberal, the modern social democratic state is essentially a benign institution – the means of ensuring justice, fairness, opportunity and equality. For the socialist and the anarchist it is essentially repressive... So for the Conservative and the Liberal, participatory community work seeks to enhance relationships between government and the people: for the anarchist participation aims to release people from their dependence on controlling institutions...'

For the Marxist or socialist he argues:

> 'participation is undoubtedly a fact of life; but not as a means of affecting redistribution so much as a means of alerting the top to pressures and alignments among lower participants so that the problem of order – social control can be effectively tackled.'

Reflecting these broad distinctions, Twelvetrees[2] (drawing on Baldock[3]) identifies two broad schools of community work thinking – the 'professional' and the 'socialist'. Though he notes the inconsistency of workers and the frequent lack of any correlation between their theoretical framework and actual practice, this distinction largely reflects the differences between the pluralist view of the state and the socialist perspective.

The former is well illustrated in the community work literature emanating from the National Institute for Social Work particularly in the Henderson, Thomas and Jones[4] notion of 'interjacence'. They say:

'We have a picture of community work (at a societal level) and community workers (at a local level) inhabiting the space between local groups and individuals and local and central organisations. In this space, community work and community workers, are not static; they move around as they are pushed and pulled by various forces that emanate either from community groups or from bureaucracies...'

Though acknowledging the fears of workers about being 'contaminated or sucked in by established professions or agencies', the idea of interjacence seems to follow a well established pluralist perspective well illustrated in the Gulbenkian report[5] of 1968 which said:

'Community work is essentially about the interrelations between people and social change, how to help people and the providers of services to bring about a more comfortable "fit" between themselves and constant change, how to survive and grow as persons in relation to others.'

In that these pluralist models of community work emphasise the servicing of the machinery of the state they reflect functionalist social theory. They do not deny that change may be needed but tend to emphasise incrementalist approaches and consensual methods. They can be contrasted with the socialist approaches which tend to be concerned about community work becoming an integral part of a state machine serving powerful vested interests. Such commentators believe that the objectives of community workers are compromised by their association with the state. In particular, Cockburn,[6] in a study highly influential in community work circles, has argued that the essential function of community work as a state- sponsored activity is to incorporate radical dissent. It does this by drawing critical community organisations into ineffectual participation in marginal areas of state decision-making. She argues that it is not just approaches to community work which are based on social pathological explanations of poverty and deprivation, and approaches based on social planning conceptions that serve state interests; methods derived from a social conflict perspective are seen as equally beneficial to the state in sustaining social equilibrium and perpetuating the power of capital. She states:[7]

> 'the state needs community workers for many reasons ... So in spite of the risk of explosive conflict (between local authority and activist groups, between officers and members and between traditional and progressive members) the local council does not always pull in the horns, nor do community workers who are into conflict always get the sack. Instead the conflict is moderated and converted, wherever possible, into a style of governance. There are two ways in which conflict in small amounts and certain contexts can help to maintain equilibrium in capitalist societies. First it can defuse a situation leading to greater and more fundamental conflicts ... Second, a degree of conflict safely contained in an electoral representative arena can redeem the idea of democracy. It makes it seem as if a genuine class struggle were taking place through the vote. Too much apathy and quietism and the system appears a charade losing its ability to legitimate the state in the people's eyes.'

Cockburn has been quoted at some length as there can be little doubt that her arguments promoted a crisis of confidence for many community workers who were disconcerted by the idea that conflict-oriented practice, based on a socialist perspective, could be seen as functional to sustaining the status quo. Community work, in Marcusian[8] terms, was to be viewed as a process of 'repressive tolerance'. Such concerns were reflected in Marxist critiques of community work. Corrigan,[9] for example, went so far as to suggest that 'the state is characterised by one of two major symbols of control in capitalist society – the tank or the community worker!'.

It was the dilemmas raised by debates around these issues which prompted Waddington[10] in 1979 to argue:

> 'the future destiny of community work, like its present and past, will be inextricably bound up with that of the state; and the crisis of community work can only be resolved by personal and collective clarifications of that relationship...'

In an exercise in futurology he predicted that the 1980s would see a cementing of the functional role of community work for the state. He argued that:[11]

'It will be their (community workers') task to manage the multiplicity of new groups and organisations which will be brought into being to engage the long term structurally unemployed and to provide the new community based social services. An increasing part of their work will involve the professional supervision of a new tier of para professional, sub professional and non-professional volunteer workers. The new community workers will act as the outreach agent, the eyes and ears, of the corporately managed major establishment institutions in helping them to better monitor their environments and manage feedback and to handle increasingly complex inter-organisational relationships... The new community workers will spend an increasing part of their work in deskbound activities and will do less direct fieldwork with clients. They will be more involved in management, in making policy and in controlling budgets and resource allocation...'

For Waddington this was not an attractive vision. He believed that 'radical dissenters' would 'need to look for the relatively autonomous spaces in the new system and to seek out the subversible areas, identifying and working on the contradictions'. Radical practice then was seen as an almost clandestine activity operating in the 'nooks and crannies' of the state. It is interesting however, that Waddington did not dismiss radical community work in the state. In this he reflects a position noted by Lambert[12] when he says 'for others, though, it remains the case that the struggle for a just socialist society is made with and through the state apparatus whose control and legitimation are by no means absolute'.

This line of argument is taken up by Blagg and Derricourt.[13] They argue that a practice based on structural class conflict theory is feasible within the state and that 'a crude anti-state view has dogged the development of community work practice'. To use Frierian[14] terminology, they seek a mode of operation within the state which promotes the liberation rather than the domestication of disadvantaged groups. They distinguish their view of community work from models derived from 'functionalist and systems theory' which have been used to 'promote consensus based community work practice'. (Here particularly they cite the work of Henderson and Thomas.[15]) They regard these latter approaches as the dominant influence in the development of community work and as reflecting the traditions of the Gulbenkian,[16] Seebohm,[17] and Skeffington[18] reports and the Home Office view of the CDP and Urban programme.[19] They justify their arguments by challenging the monolithic view of the state, arguing:[20]

'Firstly, we need to see the state as a far more complex and ambiguous formation than hitherto, not reducible either to its purely repressive apparatus or to a simple instrument of the ruling class. Secondly, we need to see the state as encompassing more than just its administrative "commanding heights".'

It might be regarded as cynical to question whether a 'new theory of the state' is needed in community work because community workers are dependent for a livelihood on employment from its resources, but as Baldock[21] has commented:

'The key boundary in community work is that on which all radical community workers stand between the world of welfare professions in which they gain the means to live and the movements for change to which they belong. To be in the welfare state but not of it is the crucial requirement made of them by the commitment to which they lay claim.'

In a study examining the Home Office CDP programme and community planning in London Docklands, Peter Marris[22] has argued that much of the debate within community work about its relationship with the state has become highly damaging to the potential influence that it could have. He suggests:

'Radicals – and increasingly, too, people more influenced by liberal, democratic traditions of reform – characteristically represent to themselves the relationships which underlie the persistence of poverty and social injustice in profoundly inhibiting and self defeating metaphors.'

He argues that there is in fact a much higher degree of common perception between sponsors of community work and its practitioners than the tenor of debate might suggest. This compatibility is to be found in the ideals towards which programmes are directed rather than in the analysis of the means by which they may be achieved. By way of example he explores the CDP programme and cites the commitment of the British Labour Party (which set it up) to egalitarian social welfare as being compatible with the ideals of CDP staff. On the other hand he suggests that the class basis of the analysis and proposals for action by CDP staff actually militated against effectiveness. He argues:[23]

'So long as government policy and community action justify themselves by the same ideals, community action has scope for influence on government's own terms, even if its ideology is in other ways radically opposed to the assumptions of government...

Movements for change are empowered by the convergence of social ideals expressed in principles of action.'

From this standpoint Marris is critical of the tendency of radical community workers to formulate responses in terms of crude and simplistic conflicts between capital and labour which fail to acknowledge the complex range of competing interest-group relationships in contemporary capitalist societies. He argues that class conflicts can be viewed in terms of the control of risks and the displacement of uncertainty onto others, the response therefore should not be to reinforce the conflicts which constantly damage the weak but to more broadly distribute risk and uncertainty thus reinforcing mutual bonds. Allied to this he argues the case for social planning, 'since planning means, essentially, controlling uncertainty'.[24]

The lesson he suggests:[25]

'is not to reject planning in favour of political struggles, but to incorporate into those struggles a demand for effective, open, collective planning, as a crucial part of carrying out any practical ideal of social justice. Otherwise, the struggle does not lead towards any resolution except competitive bargaining between different kinds of interests, and that cannot protect the weaker and more vulnerable members of society.'

The contribution offered by Marris to the debate provides community workers with an antidote to some of the crude anti-state rhetoric, and it offers a direction to the radical worker which, though pragmatic, may reduce cynicism borne of a sense of impotence. The state, particularly given its planning powers, remains a target for influence but can also be a partner for change.

Implications for Strathclyde

This brief review of some of the arguments about the location and functions of community work is of interest in relation to community work in Strathclyde in that it illustrates some of the context of debate within which the workers operate. As we have seen, their own dispositions towards the state as revealed in their views of their managers and political masters as well as the profile of their actual activities, suggests that they experience some of the conflicts outlined. However, the tensions may have less to do with a radical critique of practice held by the workers than more basic frustrations of professional identity. Indeed the profile of the work actually undertaken suggests that the practice is closer to that predicted by Waddington[26] than the more radical formulation to which the literature sometimes aspires. As Chapter 3 showed, the content of work is oriented primarily to servicing rather than issue-based action and has a particular emphasis on the provision of material and financial resources for local community groups which themselves provide local services. There is little indication in the comments of the Strathclyde workers of the kind of trenchant critique offered by CDP staff of their programme when they stated that 'the state's fight against urban deprivation has been exposed, like the "emperor's new clothes", as empty rhetoric'.[27] It may be that the workers in Strathclyde became involved at a time when community work aspirations were in any case more limited and perhaps more realistic, but the impression is of a workforce oriented more to the 'professional' than the 'socialist' school. Had CDP workers presented viable models for effective practice from their experience, this conclusion may have differed.

If community work can be categorised as belonging broadly to three schools of thought – conservative/liberal pluralist, democratic socialist and radical/Marxist – it is apparent that on this evidence the bulk of the work being undertaken falls into the first two categories.[28] Only a minority of workers espoused community action approaches while the majority were undertaking community development or community care roles. There is a relatively high level of consistency between the workers' perceptions of the work they undertook and the actual activity recorded by them. If anything, there appears to be more service-orientated and less campaigning work than workers' aspirations might imply. However, the discrepancy between hopes and realities was not excessive. With this in mind, the often negative relationship which workers appeared to experience with senior managers of the Social Work Department and the fairly negative views of the Council cannot be understood as a clash between radical aspirations and a conservative working environment. Certainly, many workers seemed to view the intentions of the Regional Council and the Social Work Department as quite conservative, but their own activities and aspirations were not in general particularly radical. The workers were commenting on their experience. This leads to questions about why the policies adopted by the Regional Council in relation to community work and deprivation, themselves reformist rather than conservative, seemed not to be reflected in the workers' view of the policy, or their experience of its management and interpretation. Put another way, were the approaches of the community workers more in touch with the intentions of the policy than those of their managers and many of the elected members with whom they interacted? Or, was there mutual misunderstanding based on a lack of appreciation of the relative roles that each party has to play? Fortunately, the evidence of change in worker attitudes between 1983 and 1989 suggests that these tensions are substantially diminishing.

Notes

1. J. Lambert, 'Political Values and Community Work Practice' in P. Curno (ed.), *Political Issues and Community Work* (London: Routledge and Kegan Paul, 1978) pp. 6–9.
2. A. Twelvetrees, *Community Work* (London: MacMillan, 1982) pp. 4–12.
3. P. Baldock, *Community Work and Social Work* (London: Routledge and Kegan Paul, 1974).
4. P. Henderson, D. Jones and D.N. Thomas, *The Boundaries of Change in Community Work* (London: George Allen and Unwin, 1980) p. 3.
5. Gulbenkian Foundation, *Community Work and Social Change* (London: Longman, 1968) p. 29.
6. C. Cockburn, *The Local State* (London: Pluto Press, 1977).
7. Ibid. p. 117.
8. H. Marcuse, *One Dimensional Man* (Harmondsworth: Penguin, 1962).
9. P. Corrigan, 'Community Work and Political Struggle – What are the Possibilities of Working on the Contradictions?' in P. Leonard, 'The Sociology of Community Action', *Sociological Review Monograph*, No. 21 (University of Keele, 1985) p. 57.

10.   P. Waddington, 'Looking Ahead – Community Work into the 1980s', *Community Development Journal*, vol.14, no.3 (October, 1979) p. 225.
11.   Ibid. p. 230.
12.   Lambert, 'Political Values', p. 9.
13.   H. Blagg and N. Derricourt, 'Why We Need to Reconstruct a Theory of the State for Community Work' in G. Craig, N. Derricourt and M. Loney, *Community Work and the State* (London: Routledge and Kegan Paul, 1982) pp. 11–22.
14.   P. Friere, *Pedagogy of the Oppressed* (Harmondsworth: Penguin, 1970).
15.   P. Henderson and D.N. Thomas, *Skills in Neighbourhood Work* (London: George Allen and Unwin, 1980).
16.   Gulbenkian, *Community Work*; and Gulbenkian Foundation, *Current Issues in Community Work* (London: Routledge and Kegan Paul, 1973).
17.   Seebohm, *Local Authority and Allied Personal Social Services* ('the Seebohm Report') (London: HMSO, 1969).
18.   A.M. Skeffington, *People and Planning*, ('the Skeffington Report') (London: HMSO, 1969).
19.   See for example, 'CDP An Official View' in R. Lees and G. Smith, *Action Research in Community Development* (London: Routledge and Kegan Paul, 1975).
20.   Blagg and Derricourt, 'Theory of State',p. 19.
21.   P. Baldock, 'The Origins of Community Work' in Henderson, Jones and Thomas, *Boundaries* p. 45.
22.   P. Marris, *Meaning and Action: Community Planning and Conceptions of Change* (London: Routledge and Kegan Paul, 1987) p. 4.
23.   Ibid. p. 157.
24.   Ibid. p. 159.
25.   Ibid. p. 160.
26.   Waddington, 'Looking Ahead'.
27.   Community Development Project, *Gilding the Ghetto: the State and the Poverty Experiments* (London: CDP Information and Intelligence Unit, 1977) p. 63.
28.   For a discussion of these schools of thought see, for example, C. McConnell, *The Community Worker as Politicisor of the Deprived* (Edinburgh: Community Education Council, 1977).

11

Community Work, Social Planning and Community Participation

The community development approach of Strathclyde Regional Council emphasises corporate working and deploys resources on the basis of systematic investigation of the spatial distribution of need. This approach has engaged the attention of both officers and elected members of the council. It has increasingly been supported by a commitment to community participation in which Area Liaison Committees have become the most significant structure. The role of community workers in relation both to social planning and community participation is, therefore, of interest.

As we have seen, particularly from the evidence from the 1983 study in Chapter 4, the levels of systematic contact between the community work staff and staff of departments other than social work was quite limited. Corporate working was not highly valued except by the more senior workers and, as Chapter 3 indicates, it was not an extensive activity. This evidence presents a picture of community work staff as relatively isolated not only in their own department but within the local authority more generally. By 1989 the emergence of the economic strategy described in the Generating Change report had precipitated a much higher level of corporate working in areas covered by major social and economic Initiatives. Worker attitudes to this are therefore important.

Although in 1983 the workers were generally characterised by a professional rather than a political orientation to community work, this did not imply high levels of interprofessional activity. Rather, the workers appeared to focus on the local communities in which they worked. Indeed the combination of this with the low level of commitment to social planning approaches (see Chapter 5) and the lack of attention to research, analysis and evaluation (see Chapter 3) presented an image of community workers in the Region reminiscent of the general view of British community work offered by Specht[1] in 1975. He stated:

> 'British community workers tend to put great value on becoming engaged with people and problems and getting into action as soon as possible. When I speak of the neglect of structure I refer to such things as systematic problem analysis, the identification of action or programme goals, the building of organisations and communication systems... and skills for evaluation and review.'

Whether the lack of engagement with organisational factors within the local authority and the tendency to be isolated from other groups of workers was a product of a conscious practice philosophy is clearly open to question. It can be argued that it may have reflected a certain arrogance on the part of community workers that they might be able to promote change independently of other workers. Twelvetrees[2] has criticised community workers for their belief that 'community work is the only way of getting done the things we want done'. He goes on to say:

> 'This in turn makes us distrustful of people in admittedly equally marginal but probably no more ineffective positions who are in some cases as committed as we are, for example, politicians, chief officers, corporate planners. Too often we see the local authority as the "enemy" and as a consequence do not exploit the expertise and commitment which sometimes exists.'

Thomas[3] has taken these arguments further by arguing for a much greater level of attention in community work to social planning approaches which would involve much higher and more systematic levels of contact between community workers and other professionals than the evidence of this study indicates to be common. In doing so however, he notes that 'community workers will be circumspect about technical skills and technologies that have largely been the monopoly of bureaucratic decision makers'. Like Specht he recognises that if community workers are to engage more at the organisational and institutional level in relation to social policy they will need skills in 'problem analysis and needs assessment, the choice of goals and priorities and the design, implementation and evaluation of programmes and interventions.'[4]

Though these skills are considered important in community work training there was little indication of their practice among this group of workers in 1983, and the 1989 audit suggests only a limited change of view. Yet this may be regarded as a fruitful avenue for community work within Strathclyde given its anti-deprivation orientation.

It should be noted that elsewhere Thomas[5] makes the point in relation to social planning skills that 'to emphasise them to the exclusion of neighbourhood organising is unhelpful, not least because it ignores the developmental goals of community work'.

The emergence from the restructuring of the Strathclyde Social Work Department in 1986 of a requirement for area teams to produce annual plans for their work provided one opportunity for community workers to develop social planning roles. The growth of major corporate social and economic development initiatives has provided another opportunity for workers in the areas concerned. In practice, the skills required of community workers are that they undertake systematic assessments of the needs of communities and the range of indigenous and external resources that may be relevant to the meeting of those needs. In any given locality there are a variety of sources of this understanding. The most significant is the community itself. However, acknowledging that communities contain many different interest groups, the worker has to develop an appreciation of the community's perception of itself which takes account of the tensions between groups based on factors such as age, sex, employment status, location of residence, length of residence, relative 'respectability', race, housing tenure, political affiliation, religion, educational attainment, and so on. Such an understanding can only come from an intimate appreciation of the lifestyles, services and institutions of the local community. There is no substitute for direct involvement with the community and its affairs. However, this means that the community worker builds up a knowledge of local conditions not simply from the members of the local community but also from those agencies and workers who provide the services consumed by the community. The worker needs to understand not only how local people see their own needs but equally how local schools, housing officials, primary health care workers, policemen, youth workers, DSS officials, public health inspectors, planning officers or social workers perceive the community and respond to it. This understanding also requires a knowledge of how voluntary and private sector agencies and religious institutions operate in the area.

In short, then, workers need to establish a well-informed view of the social, economic and political workings of the community.

There is little evidence from the diary recordings of the workers studied that they gave much attention to the systematic collection of data or analysis of data already available from a variety of sources including their own department. Their actions, it is suggested, will therefore tend to have been based on identification with particular interest groups in the community which had attracted their attention and to whose concerns they were positively disposed. Given limited resources, these may not be the ones to which attention would have been given if a more systematic assessment of needs and resources had been undertaken. To be credible in a social planning role, community workers need to be able to demonstrate the soundness of their knowledge of the community and its services, and be able to compare this with broader patterns of provision regionally and nationally.

Many community workers appear diffident about accepting this sort of role for it casts them in the mould of the expert. Rightly they are suspicious of the functioning of experts who are often seen, with some justification, as out of touch with the experiences and feelings of service consumers. The key question though, is not about expertise as such but about the way in which it is developed and used.

Development of an expert knowledge about the community should not be the basis for capturing the power to decide for people what is good for them, but a basis for a well-informed dialogue between interested parties over problems and solutions. In Marris[6] terms this is to operate in a context of 'broadly shared ideals'. This requirement presumes a genuine commitment by public authorities to accept influential participation by community interests, and the existence of a willingness to redeploy existing resources or obtain new ones. It is here that in

Strathclyde the roles of area liaison committees and corporate community initiatives come into play.

Corporate Initiatives

The 1989 audit included discussions with all the community work teams operating in areas affected by corporate economic and social development initiatives. Most notably these were the Scottish Office – New Life for Urban Scotland Partnerships in Castlemilk and Ferguslie Park; the Regional Council – Social and Economic Initiatives in Easterhouse and Drumchapel and the successor to the Glasgow Eastern Area Renewal Project, the District and Regional Council – East End Management Unit. All of these initiatives were focused on economic and social regeneration informed by resident participation.

Despite the different character of these initiatives, a remarkably consistent set of concerns emerged. They related to three main areas: public participation; the determination of the agenda for change; and the pace and complexity of the change process.

In relation to participation it was apparent that the initiatives tended to operate through representation from established and more formal community organisations. Thus more local, informal groups, which are often more responsive to immediate felt needs in the community, had difficulty creating influence. Often, too, there was little working relationship between these two kinds of groups, and thus the information flow from community representatives in initiative structures was problematic. Community workers sometimes felt pressured to work with the formal established groups though they were not necessarily in touch with many locally-defined needs and issues. It was also felt that there was sometimes an element of patronage on the part of the initiatives in the process of identifying and 'selecting' community representation which marginalised dissenting community opinion. There was also concern that levels of community participation were often very inadequate, sometimes requiring community members to represent larger populations than elected members. Significantly too, workers expressed concern about a highly formalised bureaucratic style in participation structures which inhibited local representatives unfamiliar with procedural rules. As a consequence, some teams had tried to compensate for the disadvantage experienced by community representatives by providing training opportunities.

Community work teams expressed concern that the objectives of social and economic regeneration though the initiatives were set prior to any local involvement. Similarly the methods of achieving these objectives were largely pre-determined. Hence community participation did not relate so much to the formulation of objectives as to marginal influence on the mode of implementation. Whilst it was not suggested that local people did not want economic and social regeneration, it was suggested that the 'top-down' approach placed community organisations (and the workers who supported them) in a reactive position which might generate conflict which initiative staff found difficult to understand. The conflict might arise both from direct lack of opportunity to work on locally determined priorities or from the feelings that were aroused when local people believed they were being worked on rather than with. These feelings were reinforced by mechanisms such as officer and member pre-agenda meetings for area liaison committees in which priorities for attention were determined by people who were largely external to the communities.

The third area of difficulty related to the pace and complexity of the change objectives set in initiative areas. The approach tended to be top-down, characterised by a social planning rather than a community development style. Targets were set in relatively short time scales for complex change – for example, in relation to the diversification of housing markets or industrial investment. The achievement of such changes often involved partnership with private sector agencies whose motives for involvement did not relate to principles of local democracy; highly complex negotiation between central government and the two tiers of local government; as well as inter-departmental working within local and central government. The structures which had emerged for dealing with these relationships were, almost inevitably, complex. To participate effectively, community representatives required a high level of political sophistication, a developed knowledge base and considerable self-confidence. Workers expressed concern about the lack of assistance to community organisations to develop the knowledge and skills for effective involvement. Workers also expressed concern that local people were inadequately supported to appreciate the choices which faced them and their implications. Given the pressures on the initiatives to achieve change, local people may not have had adequate time to properly understand and debate proposals before decisions were taken.

In discussions with teams operating in initiative areas, frequent reference was made to the terms of reference of community workers[7] which emphasised the 'primary focus on assisting communities to organise around locally defined needs and issues'. This was understood to require workers to operate within the priorities of local people and at their pace. This did not necessarily correspond with the initiatives expectations and workers complained that they sometimes felt pressured to 'sell' initiative proposals or to speak on behalf of community interests. They noted that the document *Helping the Community to Organise* states that 'the community workers role is never that of representing or speaking on behalf of the community nor is it to be the advocate of Council policies to the community'.[8]

The tensions between community workers and the initiatives appeared to arise primarily from differences in models and hence processes and objectives of change activity. It may not be inappropriate that different sorts of approach should be simultaneously promoted but there is a need to more clearly establish the appropriate relationships between them. It is in this context that the suggestion of more attention by community workers to social planning roles needs to be examined.

As Thomas[9] pointed out, social planning skills should not be emphasised to the exclusion of neighbourhood organising because it ignores the development of goals of community work. The evidence from the 1989 audit suggests that this is precisely the problem. Hence, any proposal that community workers should be more willing to engage in social planning roles must carry with it an equal commitment on the part of planning agencies to effective and full community participation. It is here that the role of area liaison committees is worthy of consideration. These are a primary mechanism for community participation not only in areas covered by corporate initiatives but throughout the Areas for Priority Treatment (APTs) in Strathclyde.

Area Liaison Committees

The term 'area liaison committee' (ALC) refers to local participation structures operating in APTs and providing a focus for discussion of local issues and concerns between elected members, local people and officers of the local authority. Despite this basic description, the local forms of ALC are very variable in structure, procedure, membership and style and some travel under other names such as social strategy groups or area needs group. Relationships with these bodies were extensively discussed in the 1989 audit in the meetings with teams. These discussions raised many issues; however, it is important to recognise that ALCs are not the responsibility of the Social Work Department (though it provides some of the local lead officers), but of the Chief Executive's Department.

The overwhelming feature of the evidence was the variability of forms of ALC. This reflects the absence of a prescribed format and different history and patterns of local development. Variability is not necessarily a problem in itself since structures should reflect local conditions. Nonetheless, it was difficult to discern universally agreed principles and objectives. It was also true that different formats each presented their own advantages and disadvantages. For example, in relation to participation of the community, some ALCs had open access with consequent problems of size of meetings and range and organisation of business, whilst others restricted access by formally constituting themselves with nominated representatives. The latter may have been more structured but should be criticised for unrepresentativeness, lack of flexibility and lack of capacity to respond to groups and interests not formally nominated.

Similar problems arose in terms of local authority officer representation. Those that were open sometimes became very large and unmanageable, though they might generate a sense of shared commitment to problem solving, whilst those that were closed might do the reverse. If officer representation is to be restricted, the question arises as to who are the appropriate officers to attend. More senior officers may carry the authority to respond more effectively to issues raised, though more junior ones may be most closely involved in responses and have more direct relationships in the community. One of the frequent criticisms of ALCs was that they were often unable to resolve issues raised since they did not have the authority to do so. Similarly, 'low status' lead officers such as community workers expressed difficulties in obtaining adequate responses on behalf of the ALC from departmental officers of often substantially greater seniority. As a consequence of these sorts of difficulties, some local groups took the view that ALCs were a diversion from effective means of problem resolution and did not therefore regard participation as worthwhile.

Another area of concern related to the way the lead officers played their roles. Some appeared to see the task as primarily administrative, whilst others saw it as also requiring a development role promoting and energising community activity. Though the latter was generally viewed more positively, to approach the job in this way is much more time consuming and hence often less possible for lead officers in more senior posts already carrying a wide range of responsibilities. Taking a developmental stance also requires active engagement with local organisations and lead officers involved in this way seemed more often to be criticised for partiality. In some cases, as was noted in discussion of initiative areas, direct patronage of particular interests was alleged.

The relative influence of elected members, local people and local authority officers was another major area of variability. In some cases elected members were held to use the ALC as a means of promoting their own concerns about the locality; in others the ALC was described as resembling a collective Councillors' Surgery. The most frequent concern, however, was about the influence of local authority officers. Partly this related to the role playing of lead officers who sometimes appeared to unduly influence the content of agendas. On other occasions, concern related to the behaviour of officers in meetings which effectively excluded local people. In these circumstances the ALC became a substitute for a corporate management structure rather than a mechanism for community participation and influence.

The determination of the agendas of ALCs was another theme of concern. Examples were given of the difficulties experienced in some areas by community groups wishing to place matters on an agenda. Pre-agenda meetings between the local elected member and the lead officer, excluding community representation, appeared quite common. Thus officers and members were often determining local priorities to the frustration of local groups.

A particular concern in relation to agenda content was the tendency of some departments to use the ALCs as a mechanism for getting community sanction for their plans without real consultation. The prime example concerned urban programme applications. In at least one ALC, local people had demanded that they were given proper consultation time and had refused to be party to a 'rubber stamping' exercise for local authority proposals.

Overall, ALCs appeared to be seen as a potentially valuable means for the engaging of local people with elected members and officers on a corporate basis, though a review of the most effective modes of operation and the limitations of ALCs was needed.

Concluding Comment

Whilst there may be strong arguments for community workers to engage in the social planning process and for attention to be given to the mechanisms for public participation, both present considerable dilemmas. Community work staff cannot ignore the structures; indeed Senior Community Workers may be formally required to carry roles within them, for example as lead officers to ALCs. The structures exist and impinge on community organisations so, if for no other reason, attention needs to be given to them. Some workers might argue that it is preferable to challenge rather than collaborate with them because they are not seen as effectively responding to community aspirations. Others might suggest that, given the power and resource control of corporate initiatives and of ALCs, they have to be seen as mechanisms in which local people participate. Indeed, it might be argued from this perspective that by concentrating, as workers often appear to do, on the resourcing of the community's own service initiatives and to a lesser extent, on campaigning work, it may be that community work is missing its potentially most influential role: drawing community organisations into the planning of the major public services which they consume and the planning of the regeneration of their neighbourhoods. However, given the experience of workers in relation to corporate initiatives and area liaison committees, this might be regarded as a rather simplistic and questionable conclusion. It may be more appropriate to conclude that workers should both engage with groups in these structures, whilst sustaining with them an analysis of the benefits and limitations of this involvement. Hence they will both engage in and require skills for social planning approaches but, sustaining a commitment to the principles of community development, they will be ready to work with groups outside these structures. The criterion for judgement as to which approach is appropriate will be whether local people regard the corporate structures and participation mechanisms as an effective means of responding to their locally-defined needs. Hence, social planning should not become the predominant approach, for community workers. Their primary function is to promote a basic infrastructure of effective community organisations. This will remain a perpetual task as social, economic, political and demographic changes redefine the context of practice. Within this approach, they must give central attention to educational and personal development of participants. However, in the circumstances offered by the policies of an authority like Strathclyde, community workers should be much more inclined to test out the opportunity to influence from below the policy planning process. If one of the problems is that they lack the skill to do it, this requires urgent attention to training for community work.

Notes

1. H. Specht, 'Community Development in the UK', *Policy and Politics* (Winter, 1975) p. 69.
2. A. Twelvetrees, 'A Personal View of Current Issues in Community Work', *Community Development Journal*, vol. 14, no. 3 (October 1979) p. 239.
3. D.N. Thomas, 'Community Work Social Change and Social Planning' in P. Curno (ed.), *Political Issues and Community Work* (London: Routledge and Kegan Paul, 1978) p. 247.
4. Ibid.
5. D.N. Thomas, *The Making of Community Work* (London: George Allen and Unwin, 1983) p. 109.
6. P. Marris, *Meaning and Action: Community Planning Conceptions of Change* (London: Routledge and Kegan Paul, 1987) p. 160.
7. Director of Social Work, *Helping the Community to Organise* (Strathclyde Regional Council, 1984) pp. 3–4.
8. Ibid. pp. 4–5.
9. Thomas, *Making of Community Work*.

12

Community Work and Local Community Interests

The relationship between community workers and community groups, as perceived by workers in Strathclyde Regional Social Work Department, has already been reviewed in Chapter 8. It was suggested then that the perception of community groups of the nature of their problems and the potential for change was a crucial determinant of how workers spent their time. The evidence suggested that workers had come to see the groups as trapped in parochial self-interest, competing for the time and attention of the workers and hence for a share of available resources. In such circumstances community groups may be seen as competing with one another for attention, with the result that rather than addressing wider problems of social inequality they simply alter the distribution of limited resources amongst disadvantaged groups. Equally, there is a danger that the involvement of politicians with vociferous community groups might be counter-productive to just redistributive policies. These problems are exacerbated by the degree to which the process of community work may be in conflict with its objectives.

The Process and Goals of Working with Community Groups

It has long been a tenet of faith in community work that change processes in the community start with small-scale local problems and move outwards to a broader understanding of need which places local experience in the context of an analysis of broader social inequality. Thus it is hoped that local groups will come to appreciate their position in terms of socio-economic class status, race, gender and so on. This is not to deny that there will be particular local manifestations of more generally experienced disadvantages, but it is to indicate that the educational task of community work is regarded by many workers as not only to develop skills for acting on problems, but also to develop understanding of the causes of those problems and the need to link local campaigns to broader social and political movements.

In an authority such as Strathclyde the investment in community work is in any case a part of an anti-deprivation strategy promoted by the ruling Labour group. Local experience should therefore be seen as serving a wider political strategy. Clearly, the degree of trust that community workers placed in that strategy varied considerably as the evidence of the study indicates. Similarly, as Chapter 9 suggests, the attitudes of community workers generally to the state as a potential agent of change for the disadvantaged also varies substantially. Indeed, not all community workers actually see issues of social and economic inequality as being central to community work. Nonetheless, a substantial proportion, including many of those interviewed for this study, clearly do. Since this is so, it is important to consider why the parochial tendency was so prevalent in the practice and outlook of these workers. It is here that the problems of the process and methods of community work come into play.

Whilst workers may aspire to influence broader issues, the motivation of local people to become active in their locality usually relates to problems which are experienced by their neighbours and themselves in immediate ways. The damp council house, for example, may illustrate problems in the level of public sector investment in housing nationally but, for the family which experiences it, the dampness is a problem of high fuel bills, ill health, lack of adequate space, damaged furnishings, pressures on personal relationships and so on. What motivates action is the desire to remove the immediate personal problem; what motivates collective action is the fact that many personal interests are shared in common. For that motivation to be carried into action, there has to be a belief in the potential for resolution of the problem. Even if the state of national public investment in housing is recognised as central to inequalities in housing provision, it is not likely to be seen as susceptible to change from local action. What is much more likely is that there will be local knowledge of cases where the local councillor and/or housing officials have responded to pressure from individuals or groups of people complaining about damp houses. In other words, improving your competitiveness relative to other individuals and groups is known to have produced success. It is rational self-interest, it is suggested, which draws people into community organisations to tackle local problems. While they may recognise a wider aggregate interest at city-wide or even national level, neighbourhood residents quite rationally assess the potential for change on the evidence that is available that local pressure in redirecting existing resources is easier to achieve than an overall increase. Whilst such a competitive stance may not match the objectives of many community workers, community groups may have a more pragmatic view. As O'Brien[1] puts it, 'there has been much confusion about the organisation of the poor because we have often failed to realise that service delivery systems often provide a potential basis for conflict between poor neighbourhoods'.

O'Brien also explored the problem of motivation of participation in community organisations among disadvantaged people, and suggested that altruism is not a significant factor. Rather, it is, as I have argued, mutual self-interest and the recognition that participation is likely to achieve a pay-off which would not otherwise be achieved which is central. He argues:[2]

> 'Pluralist interest group theory assumes that rational individuals will support a collective effort if they will individually benefit from that effort; however, if the benefits are available to everyone, whether or not they make a contribution, what incentive is there for a rational self-interested individual to voluntarily contribute to the costs of those efforts?'

From this position he goes on to argue that it may be necessary for community organisers to apply sanctions to ensure that benefits accrue only to those who participate. Such an approach was adopted in the Gorbals Anti-dampness Campaign. Bryant and Bryant[3] quote one of the community leaders as saying:

> 'To begin with the people's attitudes was "I won't go to the meeting because Mrs So and So is going and she'll tell me about it" – so the woman next door did the same thing and

nobody turned up. Eventually we were straight with them and wrote to them and said if they didn't come forward they'd be left out and nothing would be done for them... that was when we began to get them coming forward.'

Such a position is controversial for in effect it argues that those who act on their own self-interest are more deserving than those who do not, even though they share the same problem. Indeed, it legitimises partiality on the part of workers on the basis of the level of commitment and energy of participants. Many workers will resist this approach on ethical grounds but know, too, that the effectiveness of the community organisation may be intimately related to the rewards that participants achieve. Community workers face a dilemma, for their own aspirations for wider redistributive justice do not appear to be compatible with the motivations of community activists. They have to come to terms with this.

Community Workers and Community Groups in Strathclyde

The evidence of this study indicated a high degree of parochialism among community groups as they were perceived by community workers. This may reflect a real tension between aspirations and methods of practice. I remain concerned, however, that community workers may have succumbed too much to the local self-interests of community organisations. If they were to engage in wider social planning functions, as earlier suggested, they would be required to assess the impact of local initiatives in relation to the justice of wider social policy. Ethical dilemmas about the promotion of some community interests rather than others would have to be more openly faced. Indeed, workers might have to recognise that their energies should be directed to supporting particular kinds of initiative on the basis of just redistributive strategic social policy objectives. As in Strathclyde, these may well be defined by their employers. Community work policy in the Region appears to have been moving in this direction. The Regional Council policy statement *Social Strategy for the Eighties*[4] states:

'Strathclyde Region is not in the business of crash programmes and hopeful rhetoric – but rather a long term process of transforming the way people think about themselves and what they are capable of and of reshaping our methods of implementation accordingly... The action required was of different sorts and we have chosen in the first phase from 1976/7 to 1982/3 to concentrate on

    (a)   the encouragement of local initiatives and action
    (b)   generating greater understanding of these problems (i.e. multiple deprivation) in public agencies and commitment to move against them in appropriate ways.

We feel this was realistic and correct... Confidence has developed. Citizens are more confident of their skills, contributions and power and we are more confident about the activities which have most relevance to the people in these areas. We are now ready to move into a new phase... This phase attempts to strike a better balance between local action and central guidance: it is more detailed in its expectations of specific services but will continue to require negotiations of appropriate local development.'

This extract illustrates the increasing tendency to harness local government services including community work to the strategic priorities of the Region. This trend is also illustrated by the recent move in the Social Work Department to annually-reviewed strategic plans for the deployment of area team staff, including community workers. As a result of these trends, local community groups are likely increasingly to gain support on the basis of the congruence between their own objectives and the strategic priorities of the Regional Council. This may create tension between workers and groups when local people lack motivation to act because they foresee little chance of fulfilling their objectives. Whether community workers feel comfortable managing these tensions will depend on the degree to which they share Regional objectives, believe them to be based on an appreciative understanding of community needs, and trust the capacity and motivation of the Regions' elected members and employees to genuinely seek their achievement. From the evidence of the research this may present some problems. However, it is compatible with Marris'[5] notions of operating within a shared framework of ideals common to the state, the workers and the local community.

Having acknowledged the trend to a more directed form of community work, it would be wrong to assume that workers will not be able to influence priorities through local strategic planning processes or more significantly by the power which accrues from a sound knowledge base of a particular locality and its aspirations. In addition, more attention to analysis of community needs and appropriate responses would enhance their credibility.

There will be important choices to be made in terms of action priorities. In order to link the strategic understanding with local motivation it may be necessary to move away from the current parochial orientation and attempt to link common community interests. The 1983 research provides little evidence of such federal approaches though much more had been achieved by 1989. If this trend does not continue, the stoking-up of local demands may force the local authority to respond to competing demands in ways which run counter to the principles of equity. The local authority is recognising that market pluralism is not a basis for just social policy, and has to avoid reinforcing its own difficulties by not allowing its workers to perpetuate pluralist myths. Though there are positive signs of change from 1983 to 1989, workers still seem inclined to do so as a result of their pragmatic reactiveness to the demands placed on them by community groups. This is sometimes reinforced when managers of community workers resist the involvement of their staff in activities which cross the boundaries of districts for which they are responsible.

Community Workers and Community Activists

It is apparent both from the small number of activists with whom most workers had contact in particular communities and the regularity with which they had contact with them (see Chapter 4), that in many neighbourhoods there was a hard core of people who were extensively active in relation to community problems. Most of the Community Work Assistants were recruited from this source and the impression of a high level of voluntary involvement is reinforced by the evidence (see Chapter 2) of the voluntary activity undertaken by Community Work Assistants prior to their employment by the Regional Council. Many were already contributing levels of time to community activity equivalent to that which might be undertaken by a part-time worker. Like the groups with which they were concerned, the interests of these activists were generally highly localised. Nonetheless, the evidence suggests that a blurred distinction between the roles of activists and community work staff may not be an infrequent dilemma in community work.

Unfortunately, there was no direct evidence from the research on how the activists viewed the relationship. My own experience of community work in Strathclyde does, however, indicate some resentment that some local people have found relatively secure paid employment in work apparently not dissimilar to that undertaken by community activists. It is also the case that Community Work Assistants often find it difficult to make the transition from volunteer activist accountable only to other members of the community to community worker accountable to the local authority.

The relationship between voluntary and paid workers who share in the same tasks raises dilemmas not only in community work. The tension which the relationship creates appears to be a function of the degree of difference in role, particularly in the use of developed knowledge and skills. Where it is apparent that the paid worker makes a contribution which cannot be provided on a voluntary basis, fewer difficulties are encountered. Specialist knowledge or skills may be valued but so too is the capacity to provide a reliable service. In the case of the Community Work Assistants, it is this increased reliability and availability which, at least initially, is likely to be the most significant factor distinguishing them from voluntary activists.

The anxiety expressed by Community Work Assistants about lack of training may be evidence of a desire to develop other ways of distinguishing themselves from community activists by acquiring increased knowledge and skill. Though there are also more positive motives, the means of creating a more distinct role involves the acquisition of more developed and extensive knowledge and skills, yet ironically community work aspires to transfer skills and knowledge to community groups and agencies themselves.

There has been considerable pressure on the Regional Council by Community Work Assistants for training opportunities, both in general educational terms and in relation specifically to community work. Through day release and in-service modular courses, several Community Work Assistants have gone on to full-time professional training and become qualified.

Since 1989 they have also had access to Certificate in Social Service Training and will in future have access to Diploma in Social Work courses. Professional advancement and career development should not be derided, but it is important to recognise that there are many activists who could benefit from the same opportunities and wish to do so.

Concern with this issue was a key motivating factor in a project promoted by Ruskin College and the William Temple Foundation which drew together activists from a range of community organisations in Oxford, Manchester and Liverpool in a training and support programme. It is well worth noting the reported views of these activists:[6]

'Many participants in the programme felt that they had not received real support from institutional resource holders and that often those involved in local communities or professionals were not concerned to pass on skills and knowledge or to help people "learn to learn". This was particularly true in some situations where local people had faced a succession of "raw recruits", academically well qualified but practically inexperienced. Local leaders often spent much of their time inducting such people only to have them move on to "higher" things after a short stay.'

The evidence of this research (see Chapter 3) did not indicate significant or systematic activity by these workers to promote structured opportunities for activists to become involved in training or personal development programmes. I am aware of some good examples in Strathclyde through specialist training agencies, and nationally the Federation of Community Work Training Groups has a good record in this area, but the research suggests that this has not been a widespread activity nor part of normal community work for the workers studied. This is not to suggest that they do not see their work as performing educational functions for, as Chapter 5 in particular indicates, they did see this as significant. But they appeared to view learning as arising from the process of action rather than being offered in more formal ways.

So far I have concentrated discussion on relationships between activists and Community Work Assistants, but the issues of distinctiveness of role are also relevant to the other community work staff who appeared to tie themselves closely to the local aspirations of the community groups. I have already argued that workers should take a broader view, developing action on strategic concerns which reflect a more sophisticated analysis of social needs and priorities. This approach would create a clearer distinction between local activists and employed workers. Workers would retain support to community organisations but priorities for their activity would be based in the wider objectives of a social strategy directed towards greater social justice.

Whether this is more deserving of payment than the efforts of community activists in their own areas may still be controversial. Within current predominant social values, it will no doubt be argued that community work, as with any other occupation, can only justify itself as a paid activity if it can offer specialist knowledge and skills for which there is a market. Such a value system should be questioned, particularly if the view is taken that the British economy has reached a post-industrial state. In other words, if the economy no longer needs or creates full employment, and communities have substantial proportions of able people no longer in work, should we not reassess the contribution of voluntary work to community well-being and give it monetary value? This may sound utopian but in an increasingly unequal society which produces massive social needs and problems in disadvantaged areas, there is a real danger that community care activities in particular are being developed through community workers on the basis of the assumed availability of voluntary labour. Resources in terms of buildings, equipment and organisers are being provided by the state but the services are provided by volunteers whose only reward is personal fulfilment or relief from the stresses of unemployment. We are becoming a society where those who are financially secure are encouraged to buy their social services in the private market whilst the unemployed and low paid are left to rely on under-resourced public services which they are then encouraged to supplement by their own efforts.

If community work is genuinely concerned about justice, more attention should perhaps be given to the contradictions between its own professional aspirations and the roles in which it is engaging others to work on a voluntary basis. If equal pay for equal work is a principle of equal opportunities legislation, and trade union struggles, where does the unemployed, voluntary community activist stand?

Interestingly the Regional Social Strategy sees the development of community initiatives as a means to empower of communities in relation to their own needs. This is related to a philosophy of positive discrimination which has seen a shift in the balance of local authority welfare resources to the most disadvantaged neighbourhoods. Yet in some respects the product in terms of community self-help, though described in different language, might be applauded by welfare minimalists of the New Right whose arguments Brenton[7] suggests are 'motivated by the desire to restrict government responsibility and cut welfare spending'. She goes on:[8]

'They are directed towards a substitution which offers substantial cost advantages, and are, therefore, only realisable in terms of volunteer rather than paid labour, and unpaid, informal care by women rather than collectively organised services. They envisage the return of responsibility for "self-help" to individuals and communities, and imply the possibility of a radical dismantling of the personal social services through a gradual process of resource starvation.'

Strathclyde Regional Council[9] is clearly committed in its policy to 'improve services for the most needy even if central government cutbacks mean that this requires directing resources from elsewhere'. Later, the *Social Strategy for the Eighties* document states in relation to evaluation of the strategy: 'we would therefore apply two tests to the last six years: the take-up of services and community action.'[10]

Whilst the first of these criteria would clearly not meet the requirements of welfare minimalists, the second would, in so far as this research shows it to be extensively focused on local self-help services provided through voluntary labour. Inadvertently, the conditions may be created in which, if public sector welfare spending continues to be cut back, there will be a more adequate community-based welfare infrastructure which could be used to justify an even more residual form of state welfare provision. This has to be guarded against. The issues need to be openly faced with community groups and activists. The argument that there should be more opportunities for citizens to work voluntarily in public services, as an expression of fraternity and the rights and obligations of citizenship[11] may have validity in a situation where such action is based on free choice, but it does not hold when the burden of caring is deliberately thrust back on self help. The latter is the logic of recent government thinking. To quote John Moore in a speech to the Conservative Party Conference of 1987:[12]

> 'We have a different vision of what it means to "protect and promote economic and social welfare" in this country. We believe that dependence in the long run decreases human freedom. We believe the well being of individuals is protected and promoted when they are helped to be independent, to use their talents to take care of themselves and their families and to achieve things on their own...
>
> Therefore the next step forward in the long evolutionary march of the welfare state in Britain is away from dependence toward independence.
>
> This is, I submit, the principle which should guide the formation of social policy into the next century.'

Community work beware!

Notes

1. D.J. O'Brien, *Neighbourhood Organisation and Interest Group Processes* (Princeton University Press, 1975) p. 11.
2. Ibid. pp. 21–22.
3. B. Bryant and R. Bryant, *Change and Conflict – a Study of Community Work in Glasgow* (Aberdeen University Press, 1982) p. 68.
4. Strathclyde Regional Council, *Social Strategy for the Eighties* (1984) p. 49.
5. P. Marris, *Meaning and Action – Community Planning and Conceptions of Change* (London: Routledge and Kegan Paul, 1987).
6. *Communities in Crisis – a Resource Programme for Local Organisations and Leaders* (Ruskin College, Oxford and William Temple Foundation, 1985) p. 54.
7. M. Brenton, *The Voluntary Sector in British Social Services* (London: Longman, 1985) p. 211.
8. Ibid. p. 212.
9. Strathclyde Regional Council, *Social Strategy*, p. 2.
10. Ibid. p. 5.
11. For a discussion of voluntary work and citizenship, see *Encouraging Citizenship – Report of the Commission on Citizenship* (London: HMSO, 1990).
12. Edited version of speech by John Moore, *Guardian*, 2 October 1987.

13

The Employment of Community Workers

The position of community workers in Strathclyde Regional Council reflects the common pattern, illustrated by Francis et al,[1] in which workers are employed in departments or agencies which carry much wider functions than community work. Here they find themselves in a minority, relative to the mainstream activities of the department – in the case of the workers studied here, substantially outnumbered by social work staff of various kinds. Whilst their employing agency suggests that all its employees should take a community development approach to their work, this is a mixed blessing. On the one hand it legitimises community work values and styles of working, on the other it suggests that it may not be a specialist function. This ambivalence about the role and status of community workers has significance for their sense of professional identity and security.

An important question underlying this uncertainty is whether the objectives of community work are most effectively carried by specialist community workers or by the development of community work skills by practitioners in a wide range of public services. It can be argued that the organisational nature of local authorities indicates that most community needs are seen as primarily the responsibility of particular departments. Thus, problems with schooling are located with the education department, problems of housing with the housing department and so on. This may be organisationally convenient but it does not necessarily reflect consumer experience of need. Problems of housing overcrowding in a community for example, may create household stresses which affect health, educational performance of children, and marital relationships. In addition, they might produce conflicts between neighbours and are probably an indicator of poverty. The problem, therefore, potentially involves many departments, – housing, education, social work, the police, health and so on. Each department may view the need from the particular aspect with which it is presented but is in fact only responding to a single dimension of a multi-faceted problem.[2]

The deficiencies of this approach are clearly recognised by many local authorities and in Strathclyde it is a fundamental concern of its social strategy to seek not only to promote collaborative practice between its own departments, but also those of the District Councils. It has developed in-service training packages specifically designed to foster this collaborative approach and has involved local community organisations as well as professional staff. All this raises questions as to where community work staff should be located and whether they have a specialist or generalist function. It may even lead to questions about whether local authorities should directly employ community workers themselves.

Separation or Integration

If the basic purpose of employing community workers is seen, as in Strathclyde, as 'assisting communities to organise around locally defined needs and issues'[3] but those transcend the responsibilities of any one department, there is clearly a potential problem if community workers are employed in particular service departments and constrained by the limitations of the departmental remit. This argument has been used often in local authorities to place a community development function within chief executive's departments which have a corporate overview of policies but no direct service delivery function. It has also been an argument for a separate department of community work. Strathclyde has exhibited considerable ambivalence in relation to the location of community work staff.

The ambivalence on the part of Strathclyde Regional Council as an employer of community workers can be illustrated in a number of ways. Most significantly, perhaps, when it undertook its policy review of community work in 1976, it examined community work as a part of the functions of the Social Work Department, the Education Department, and, given the role of the Community Involvement Branch, the Police. Whilst it was able to identify common principles and objectives for community work practice in these different contexts, it did not go on to suggest that community work required independent departmental status. Operational control of the Police was in any case outside their powers, but an independent Department of Community Development within the local authority was considered but rejected. Three grounds were stated: that there were 'in existence fairly strong departmental loyalties which would tend to militate against any smooth integration'; that there would be considerable additional costs; and most significantly, that they saw the specialist community workers as the means of bringing about a more community oriented practice in the service departments.[4] To quote:[5]

'Community work is essentially two pronged, the worker should be concerned not only with meeting the needs of the groups with which he is working in the community, but also with working within his own department so as to improve its internal knowledge of community problems and aspirations, in the hope of ultimately modifying its practices and policies in ways which are to the community's advantage.'

The evidence from the 1983 study indicated the latter could be difficult to realise. In the Social Work Department at least, workers appeared (see Chapter 5) not to see influencing of their own department as a high priority, they did not generally regard their social work colleagues or managers as open to such influence (see Chapter 6), and they viewed the groups with whom they worked as resenting time spent on this type of activity (see Chapter 8). The workers experienced location in a more established host discipline with defined statutory functions, as threatening to the development of their role. Community work itself was felt to have become fragmented through the lack of clear organisational mechanisms within the agency by which workers could share their concerns, undertake collective evaluation of practice or communicate its lessons.

Whilst the review group did not establish an independent department, it did establish a Community Development Services Committee to relate to community work matters in all departments. However, the 1983 evidence did not suggest that this compensated for the lack of professional identity arising from the distribution of workers in broader host disciplines. The limited impact of the strategy of influence through dispersion of community work staff was to an extent recognised by the Regional Council in its policy document Social Strategy for the Eighties.[6] It stated:

> 'Our formal political commitment has never wavered but we have to recognise that many staff did not know that we had a policy, let alone what it meant for them. Many of those who did saw it as a charitable gesture, in terms of dropping a few crumbs once the rest had had their fill...Such perceptions reflect the "blaming the victims" views deeply entrenched in society as a whole – as well as judgements about the "peripheral" nature of the Region's strategy in relation to the "real" work of departments.'

It went on to say with reference to the use of urban aid money as a major source of funding for the strategy that 'this has encouraged the view that the deprivation strategy is something to be left to Social Work – and within that, to community workers. This is a grave misconception.'[7]

To some extent, especially in relation to the Social Work Department, these judgements may have been premature. By 1989, as Chapter 6 indicates, the evidence was much more encouraging. Though all the difficulties identified in 1983 were still present, they were not nearly as widely reported. The elevation of significant numbers of former community work staff to more senior management positions, in particular, appeared to have infused a wider community development perspective in practice, though this was by no means universal. It is also the case that more recently trained social workers often influenced by the ideas underlying community social work are more attuned to a community development perspective in practice and are hence more inclined towards collaborative working. Both these factors suggest that the objective of diffusion of a community development philosophy by dispersion of specialist staff may not be unattainable, but that it is likely to be very slow. Indeed, it may depend on a shift of dominant professional ideology which can only be achieved with the career advancement of a new generation of staff replacing the old order. If this is so, patience as well as persistence will need to be the hallmarks of those who wish to achieve this change.

Whilst the Council may regard the view that the deprivation strategy is a primary responsibility of community workers, especially those in the Social Work Department, as 'a grave misconception', the fact that it has arisen at all might be seen as an argument against specialist community work staff. From this viewpoint, the emphasis would be placed on all departmental staff developing community work skills and performing their roles with a concern for the promotion of local organisation around community problems as the policy review group of 1976 suggested. To genuinely reflect community concerns, this would necessarily involve not only the promotion of organisations whose objectives were compatible with those of the departments of the local authorities, but also support to groups critical of the services provided. I question whether such a proposition is realistic. In particular, it would require the development in all staff of an understanding of, and commitment to, the complex and time-consuming process of developing and supporting community initiative. As has been noted in relation to social work, most managers and workers lack substantial knowledge or developed skills in community work, let alone the motivation or time to undertake these tasks. Without a role model, how are they to acquire this perspective and associated skills?

If this is true of the department which the Regional Council has seen as being most associated with its social strategy, it is generally doubtful whether this approach could work even with substantial investment in retraining and education to challenge established professional styles and values. Dismissing the argument that specialist workers are not required does not resolve the problems which arise when the existence of specialist workers is used by other staff to absolve themselves from engagement in the community development styles of working on which the social strategy depends. For the approach to be effective requires a corporate commitment of local authority staff to these styles of working.

As Hambleton has commented:[8]

'it is inevitable that new initiatives will be faced with formidable opposition from entrenched interests.... Opposition may take the form of hostile resistance, overt or underground, but a more subtle and probably widespread response is to absorb the threat – to defuse, dilute and redirect the energies originally directed towards change.'

It is this subtle resistance which is most difficult to combat, and it was the fear of many community workers that the emergence of a commitment to a more community-oriented form of social work practice might in fact represent an absorption and dilution of the objectives of both community work and the social strategy. However, much of the fear about the recent restructuring of the Social Work Department, in which community work staff have been much more closely integrated with the work of the area teams, has dissipated. Increasingly, workers identify opportunities for change, and community development perspectives are more apparent in the practices of the department.

To a considerable extent, the establishment of effective influence in the Social Work Department resolves the question as to whether it would be better if community workers were all placed in a separate department or located in the Chief Executive's Department. Though the influence of dispersion in a service department may be slow it is essential, for community development to flourish, for its values and practices to be widely appreciated in mainstream practice. Neither a separate department nor a Chief Executive's Department, which is not primarily oriented to provision of direct services to the public, would as adequately enable the necessary process of diffusion of ideas and practices.

As we have seen, there are community development staff in the Chief Executive's Department in Strathclyde. Though there is a small unit concerned with unemployment, the primary roles of these staff are associated with corporate social and economic initiatives (discussed in the previous chapter). The Department also services the divisional community development committees and is responsible for area liaison committees. The Department sustains a strategic policy overview in relation to social and economic strategy. The separation of these functions in departmental terms from the local empowerment functions of other community work staff is important. In particular, it relieves the likelihood of field workers feeling pressured to respond to locally-expressed need only in terms which reflect strategic priorities.

Where Chief Executive's Department staff have a direct development function in initiative areas, this operates primarily from a top-down social planning practice model. Whilst I have argued that staff in the Social Work Department should be more open to engagement in social planning approaches, I have also made it clear that this should not be at the expense of neighbourhood empowerment work. If community work was solely in the hands of one department, I would suggest that a necessary diversity of approaches would be difficult to sustain. For this reason, it is appropriate that a plurality of means of promoting community work should be maintained.

Wherever community work staff are located, the strength of their influence on colleagues in their host setting might be greater if the workers had a clearer professional and organisational identity within the local authority. They appear to feel that they are operating on the 'coat tails' of other disciplines and have little formal opportunity to engage with one another in pursuit of a clearer sense of their particular knowledge and skill base. Such development work has largely been left to informal and sporadic self-help activity by workers independent of their employers. In relation to the Social Work Department, there is little evidence from the discussion of what the workers do (see Chapter 3) that much attention was being given to these issues or, from the more recent 1989 evidence, that sufficient is being done in the area of in-service training.

Alternative Approaches

There are alternative responses to these organisational difficulties. One would be to employ community work staff at 'arms length' from the local authority itself. In such an approach the authority would commit a similar level of resources but invite one or more third parties to take responsibility for community workers. The third party could either be a professional agency or a local community organisation and would contract to work beyond the organisational constraints of local government convention.

Third sector professional agencies are commonly and often very successfully used for demonstration projects; however, I am unaware of their use in relation to long-term strategically-planned programmes intended to generate corporate commitment to partnership with local communities. Such a model applied in relation to the level of investment in Strathclyde would be unique.

Certain local third sector agencies in Strathclyde already contract to undertake work fulfilling particular objectives of the social strategy. The most substantial example is Strathclyde Community Business Ltd which promotes community enterprise work in the Region with substantial support from but also accountability to the Council.

Community business/enterprise development work is a specialised area, deserving of substantial support but needing to be seen only as a part of the overall range of approaches required. Nonetheless, it is arguable that if community business development can be promoted through a third party agency in a way which fulfils local authority policy aspirations, so too could other areas of practice. It is possible to envisage similar quasi-independent agencies focusing on themes such as health, housing, womens issues, ethnic minorities or community work training. Such a model has attractions in that agencies could be contracted to focus work on strategic priorities of the Regional Social Policy. Targeted in this way it might be easier to evaluate the impact of the investment.

There are, however, considerable weaknesses to such an approach. Firstly, it would reflect the convention of compartmentalising people's needs for the organisational convenience of the service agency, thus ignoring the interrelationships between needs. For example, health is affected by lack of jobs and poor housing but whose responsibility would such concerns be? Secondly, the contracting out of responsibility in this way would be likely to reduce the impact of community development principles on mainstream departments of the local authority. Thirdly, especially under the financial pressures experienced by local authorities in recent years, such agencies would be very vulnerable. Voluntary agencies have argued for years that they are hamstrung by the tendency of local authorities (and others) only to commit themselves to short-term funding when the needs to be met require long-term commitment. Negotiating satisfactory contracts which realistically acknowledge the time-scales required to promote effective change is difficult.

The last two weaknesses to a contracted-out approach would apply equally to a model which involved a generic community work agency as to a series of third party agencies with responsibility in relation to particular strategic priorities. The notion of an agreement with a single third party agency, however, contains further risks. There would be likely to be fears about transferring the sort of investment currently given to community work to a large-scale agency only indirectly accountable to the authority. It should not be assumed that the accountability structures of such third party agencies are necessarily more desirable than those of local authorities, especially from the viewpoint of members of local communities. For all the weaknesses of local representative democracy and local government bureaucracy, there is a degree of access to elected representatives and political authority over professional practice which may be more effective than the mechanisms offered by the alternatives.

It might be argued that if community work is to truly reflect democratic principles, it ought to be neither local authorities or third sector professional agencies but the community itself which employs community workers. In this approach local authorities would fund independent local community organisations.

This model has considerable ideological attractions but may also have both dangers and limitations. Many of these are the same as those arising for professional third sector agencies but there are additional factors. There is the difficulty of determining which organisations will be favoured with what level of resources. Clearly, to sustain accountability for use of public funds, community organisations would have to be properly constituted with clear statements and objectives. However, local communities contain diverse interests and often experience internal conflicts which would require assessment. Community organisations are also often motivated by specific issues for particular time periods. Such organisations would not be suitable vehicles for deploying community workers whose role is to respond equitably to a range of community needs. Thus it would be necessary to work through multi-functional organisations with some degree of stability. Such organisations may, however, have a tendency to stagnation often resulting from a developing monopoly of power in the hands of few, long-established active members.

Despite these difficulties, interesting examples have existed for some time and new ones, such as Drumchapel Community Organisations Council, are emerging. The potential of the approach deserves proper examination and it may be desirable in any case to promote a plurality of means of employing community work staff.

Concluding Comment

My overall reaction to the 'arms length' arguments in relation both to third sector professional agencies and community organisations is to proceed with caution, to concentrate on demonstration, and to monitor and evaluate carefully. There is no doubt that skilled agencies exist to take on such roles, and their intervention can be catalytic. There are also some suitable local community organisations. I am not convinced, however, that they can or should be seen as a long-term substitute for commitment by local government itself. In my view, community work is a mechanism to strengthen local democracy – not a substitute for it. If its influence is not sustained within local government, community work may perceive itself as a substitute, and open up irresolvable conflicts with its most likely source of funding support.

As we have seen, community workers within the Social Work Department have expressed many frustrations, and they may not have delivered all that could have been expected of them. But the potential for long-term change of attitude to partnership with consumers is likely to emerge from within the department, rather than outside. Particular strategic objectives may be served best by contracting out demonstration programmes, sometimes of quite large scale, to third party agencies but such contracts must start from the recognition that demonstration only has value if account is taken of the lessons learned, however uncomfortable. From the outset, therefore, as part of such contracts, mechanisms by which learning will be disseminated and transferred to mainstream practice must be clear. Agencies wishing to enter into such contracts with local authorities will require a pragmatic approach which acknowledges the complexities and pace of incremental change in large bureaucratic structures subject to established political and professional conventions.

Despite the potential for contracting out some elements, community work remains an essential responsibility for the local authority itself. Community workers need to acknowledge and work more effectively to address the opportunities raised by their location. The key messages which they are in a position to present to other local authority staff concern the need to listen to consumers and to respond to their interests in an empowering manner.

There is evidence from the 1989 audit that workers in the Strathclyde Social Work Department are beginning to do this much more effectively. There are strong indications that a more mature and sophisticated approach is developing which will enhance the authority of community workers in relationships with their colleagues. The concentration of community workers in the Region and their relative security has placed them in a strong position to establish their role as an important local government function.

Notes

1. D. Francis, P. Henderson and D.N. Thomas, *A Survey of Community Workers in the UK* (London: National Institute for Social Work, 1984).

2. For a discussion of some of these issues see, for example, D. Stewart et al, *Local Government: Approaches to Urban Deprivation*, Occasional Paper No. 1 (London: Home Office Urban Deprivation Unit, 1976).

3. Director of Social Work, *Helping the Community to Organise* (Strathclyde Regional Council, 1984) para. 3.4.

4. A. Worthington, *Policy Review Group on Community Development Services* ('the Worthington Report') (Strathclyde Regional Council, 1978) p. 28.

5. Ibid.

6. Strathclyde Regional Council, *Social Strategy for the Eighties* (1984) p. 32.

7. Ibid.

8. R. Hambleton, 'Implementing Inner City Policy: Reflections from Experience', *Policy and Politics*, vol. 9 (1981) pp. 64–65.

14

Key Lessons

The purpose of this book is not simply to recount and reflect upon the developments of the community work role in an anti-deprivation strategy in one local authority, albeit the most substantial of its kind in British local government. It has been written to provide pointers to good policy and practice which are transferrable to other settings. Many of these should be evident from the text. This final Chapter does not discuss new material but attempts to draw together some of the major lessons to which attention should be given.

There are different audiences for these lessons. They include community workers themselves, local authorities as employers and managers of community workers, other workers involved in community development strategies and community work trainers. The lessons have been clustered into four sets. The first relates to the lessons for local authority politicians and officers as employers and managers concerned with community development as an element of their social or economic strategies. The second set concerns the approaches of community workers to their own professional practice. The third focuses on the frequent setting of community workers within broader host disciplines and relates to means of establishing compatible and productive working relationships with colleagues. The final set explores lessons for trainers.

Lessons for Local Authorities as Employers and Managers

- Community work provides a great opportunity for radical alliances of professional, political and community interests to promote redistributive, anti-deprivation policies and practices.

- Community work is a useful means to counteract centralising tendencies in local and central government which make them more remote from the people they serve.
- Community work can help counteract the confusion experienced by consumers in relating to functionally fragmented provision of local and central government services.
- It is a legitimate function of community work to work with politicians and local community organisations to challenge the subversion of open political decision making by professional administrators.
- Community workers should not be made the spearhead of complex social changes for which their methods are inappropriate and should not be made the scapegoat for any failings of social policy on this basis.
- The political authority of the local authority employer to set policies for community work needs to be fully acknowledged by its practitioners. However, politicians should not expect or get uncritical acceptance of policy.
- Goals set for community work should be based on a realistic assessment of the potential of the method to achieve the desired changes. This applies both to policy makers and practitioners.
- Community work should be seen as just one in a range of methods of promoting social change which counteract the problems of people in disadvantaged communities.
- The application of community work techniques must not be seen as the exclusive province of community workers.
- In-service training in community-based approaches to social problems is needed for all local authority workers if they are to be able to contribute to a community development-oriented social strategy. It is most urgently needed for non-specialist managers of community workers.
- Though wider strategic social policy concerns should have more influence in community work activity, there are very significant ameliorations of a variety of social problems which can be achieved through the development of the latent skills and talents of local people in community care activity in their own communities.
- However, particularly in communities characterised by substantial and long-term unemployment, volunteer community activists should not be exploited as a cheap source of labour for community care projects.

- Equally, local authorities, community workers and community organisations need to guard against undermining public welfare services by substitution of them by the voluntary community activities promoted through community work. Pressure created by public expenditure cuts should not be allowed to encourage such substitution.
- The potential for contracting out community work functions to non-statutory agencies should be given proper consideration. However, it should be recognised that this cannot be a substitute for institutional commitment by local authorities to empowering their consumers through application of community development principles.
- The potential for contracting out community work functions to local community organisations should be explored. Experiments of this kind should be effectively monitored and evaluated.
- The roles of community workers, as brokers and intermediaries in promoting community influence on, and participation in, local affairs should be acknowledged as legitimately involving them in political processes. Such roles overlap with those of elected members and should be recognised as an inevitable consequence of employing community workers. They should not, however, use this position to subvert, but to promote, effective local representative politics.
- Good relations between community workers and politicians will only be sustained if they both carry their roles in ways which reflect agreed strategic redistributive local authority policies.
- It is appropriate that the local authorities should employ workers broadly associated with reformist approaches to practice.

Lessons for Community Workers

- The political authority of the local authority employer to set policies for community development should be fully acknowledged by its practitioners. However, politicians should not expect or get uncritical acceptance of policy.
- Community workers cannot justify their interventions on the basis of their personal dispositions towards particular interests that have attracted their attention.

- Community workers' interventions should be justified within an analysis of need. This analysis should be reflected in the stated objectives and policies of their local authority employers. In these circumstances the priorities of the policies and the practice of the workers should be compatible.
- Community workers should become less parochial in their approaches to practice and engage in more inter-organisational and inter-neighbourhood work.
- Community workers need to give much greater attention to systematic investigation of social conditions in the communities in which they work.
- Community workers must show more inclination to place the local conditions with which they work in the context of broader patterns of need and service provision.
- Community workers need to give much greater attention to analysis, reflection, and evaluation of their work and apply this to the planning of their interventions.
- Community workers need to give much greater attention to explaining the roles and purposes of their activities to both workers in other professions and politicians.
- Community workers should demonstrate more commitment to the development of their own expertise, not as an exclusive commodity but as a means of serving the interests of disadvantaged people.
- Community workers need to assert their particular professional contribution and present themselves in an effective way to outside audiences.
- Community workers should recognise that the values of community empowerment are not incompatible with the organised expression of community work opinion and develop a professional organisation which speaks with authority for community work and its consumers.
- Community workers should not disguise the shortcomings of their performance which are their responsibility by displacing the blame onto others, most particularly their managers, politicians or the community organisations with which they work.
- Community workers should reduce their isolation from other local authority staff and give more attention to promoting relationships which foster the engagement of other disciplines in community development.

- Community workers should develop a more sophisticated appreciation of the work of other professions and departments and of the local authority as a whole.
- Community workers should give full recognition to the validity of non-community work methods which achieve the same ends as they seek.
- Community workers should recognise and work more extensively in alliances with other professions who have expertise to offer in tackling community problems.
- If community workers are to give more attention to social planning approaches, improved relations with and understanding of other disciplines are imperative.
- Community workers need to develop a more sophisticated understanding of the complexity of the roles of elected members and their relationships with local government officers.
- Community workers should give attention to sustaining their relationships with elected members which engage them in the debate of local problems before they are presented for decisions. This is particularly important in relation to proposals of a controversial nature or presented by unpopular minority interests.
- Community groups appear to be primarily motivated by self interest and local concerns. Community workers have succumbed too much to these interests and should not regard local organisations as having sovereign authority over workers activities.
- Community workers need to negotiate local interests in the context of wider social policy objectives aimed at just distribution of resources. Their activities should serve, not distort, these objectives.
- Community workers should become more engaged in collaborative action between community groups directed towards strategic policy objectives.
- Federal campaigns by community organisations should be linked to parallel action by the local authority itself or other pressure groups including trade unions and voluntary organisations.
- Whilst greater emphasis should be given to social planning and inter-neighbourhood work, community workers should retain a basic concern with promoting an effective infrastruc-

ture of service and campaigning organisations in disadvantaged communities.

- Community workers should give more attention to assisting community organisations to gain skills to test the potential of community participation opportunities.

Lessons for Community Work and other Host Disciplines

- Community work has a legitimate claim to be a professional discipline in its own right, and though it may operate in a range of host departments, requires organisational arrangements which provide scope for the effective development of its particular contribution.

- If community work staff are employed in host departments rather than in a separate department, there is a need to ensure that work can still take place across departmental boundaries.

- Where an employing authority sets community development as an underlying principle, community workers are entitled to expect all of their colleagues and managers to operate in ways compatible with these objectives.

- Community workers, their managers and colleagues in their host departments should explore the reasons for the tensions between them and develop more compatible working relationships.

- For community workers to work compatibly with their colleagues they should seek common principles of operation. These should include: understanding need from the consumer perspective; recognising and responding to both private troubles and public issues and seeing them as interconnected; seeking to liberate, not domesticate, community resources and energies; and promoting, as far as is possible, a preventive approach to social problems.

- Where community work and other staff are working towards common objectives there is the basis for collaborative practice and evaluation.

- Community workers should regard their own employing departments as a much more significant focus for their change efforts.

- Community work and social work in particular have common cause to improve their knowledge and skills for collaborative practice.
- In order that social work agencies as host departments are better able to appreciate and work with community workers, all social work qualifying training courses should give substantial attention to teaching and practice of community work as a social work method and as a method in its own right. Similar attention is required in other disciplines.

Lessons for Trainers

- The quality and focus of pre-service training for community work requires urgent review.
- General areas of learning which appear to require increased attention in training for community work are study; analysis; evaluation; communication; inter-organisational work; political and educational skills; management and organisation of self in an isolated work role; planning skills; skills for collaborative work with other disciplines; knowledge of central and local government policy processes.
- The specific need for community workers to develop community-based social planning roles requires increased skills in data collection and analysis of local communities and their social, political, and economic characteristics and needs. It also requires the ability to understand and interpret evidence from other agencies, and skills for collaborative practice between agencies.
- Given current constraints on public expenditure in higher education, it may be more productive to focus attention on improving the community work dimensions of non-specialist training courses than attempting to promote specialist courses. This applies particularly to the new Diploma in Social Work and community education courses.
- Further development and experimentation with apprenticeship schemes and agency/college partnerships should be undertaken.
- More specifically, partnership arrangements between a number of employers and colleges for resourcing regional community work training, research and consultancy agencies should be explored.

- Increased attention is required to in-service training for all local authority workers who are expected to contribute to community development-based social strategies.
- Much more attention should be given to training opportunities for voluntary community activists.
- In the light of the blurred distinctions of work between many community activists and paid community workers, parallel and joint training and development programmes should be given more attention.

Bibliography

Association of Metropolitan Authorities. *Community Development – the Local Authority Role* (1989).

Abel-Smith, B. and Townsend, P. *The Poor and the Poorest* (London: Bell, 1965).

Alexander, K.J.W. *Adult Education: the Challenge of Change* ('the Alexander Report') (Edinburgh: HMSO, 1975).

Baldock, P. *Community Work and Social Work* (London: Routledge and Kegan Paul, 1974).

————. 'Community Work and the Social Services Departments' in Craig, G., Derricourt, N. and Loney M. *Community Work and the State* (London: Routledge and Kegan Paul, 1982).

————. 'The Origins of Community Work' in Henderson, P., Jones, D. and Thomas, D.N. *The Boundaries of Change in Community Work* (London: George Allen and Unwin, 1980).

Barr, A. 'Practice Models and Training Issues' in Bidwell, L. and McConnell, C. *Community Education and Community Development* (Dundee College of Education, 1982).

————. 'The Practice of Neighbourhood Community Work', *Papers in Community Studies*, No. 12 (University of York, 1977).

Benington, J. 'The Flaw in the Pluralist Heaven: Changing Strategies in the Coventry C.D.P' in Lees, R. and Smith, G. *Action – Research in Community Development* (London: Routledge and Kegan Paul, 1975).

Blagg, H. and Derricourt, N. 'Why we Need to Reconstruct a Theory of the State for Community Work' in Craig, G., Derricourt, N. and Loney, M. *Community Work and the State* (London: Routledge and Kegan Paul, 1982).

Boaden, N., Goldsmith, M., Hampton, W. and Stringer P. *Public Participation in Local Services* (London: Longman, 1982).

Brenton, M. *The Voluntary Sector in British Social Services* (London: Longman, 1985).

Bryant, B. and Bryant, R. *Change and Conflict – a Study of Community Work in Glasgow* (Aberdeen University Press, 1982).

Butcher, H., Collis, P., Glen, A. and Sills, P. *Community Groups in Action – Case Studies and Analysis* (London: Routledge and Kegan Paul, 1980).

'CDP An Official View' in Lees, R. and Smith, G. *Action Research in Community Development* (London: Routledge and Kegan Paul, 1975).

Central Council for Education and Training in Social Work. *Social Work Curriculum Study – the Teaching of Community Work* (1974).

Cheetham, J. and Hill, M.J. 'Community Work: Social Realities and Ethical Dilemmas', *British Journal of Social Work*, vol. 3, no. 3 (1973) reprinted in Henderson, P. and Thomas, D.N. *Readings in Community Work* (London: George Allen and Unwin, 1981).

Cliffe, D. *Community Work in Leicester* (Leicester: Centre for Mass Communication Research, University of Leicester, 1985).

Cockburn, C. *The Local State* (London: Pluto Press, 1977).

Communities in Crisis – a Resource Programme for Local Organisations and Leaders (Oxford: Ruskin College, Oxford and William Temple Foundation, 1985).

Community Development Journal ('Consumer Action and Community Development') (Autumn 1989).

Community Development Project. *Gilding the Ghetto: the State and the Poverty Experiments* (London: CDP Information and Intelligence Unit, 1977).

Consumers Guide to Community Work (London: Association of Community Workers with National Consumer Council, 1987).

Corina, L. 'Local Government Decision Making – Some Influences on Elected Members' Role Playing', *Papers in Community Studies*, No. 2. (Department of Social Administration and Social Work, University of York, 1975).

Corrigan, P. 'Community Work and Political Struggle – What are the Possibilities of Working on the Contradictions?' in Leonard, P. 'The Sociology of Community Action', *Sociological Review Monograph*, No. 21 (University of Keele, 1985).

Darke, R. and Walker, R. *Local Government and the Public* (London: Leonard Hill, 1977).

Davies, C. and Crousaz, D. *Local Authority Community Work – Realities of Practice* (London: HMSO, 1982).

Director of Social Work. *Helping the Community to Organise* (Strathclyde Regional Council, 1984).

Encouraging Citizenship – Report of the Commission on Citizenship (London: HMSO, 1990).

Etzioni, A. *The Semi-professions and their Organisation – Teachers, Nurses, Social Workers* (New York: The Free Press, 1969).

Francis, D., Henderson, P. and Thomas, D.N. *A Survey of Community Workers in the UK* (London: National Institute for Social Work, 1984).

Friere, P. *Pedagogy of the Oppressed* (Harmondsworth: Penguin, 1970).

The Gulbenkian Foundation. *Community Work and Social Change* (London: Longman, 1968).

—————. *Current Issues in Community Work* (London: Routledge and Kegan Paul, 1973).

Hall, P., Land, H., Parker, R. and Webb, A. *Change, Choice and Conflict in Social Policy* (London: Heinemann, 1975).

Hambleton, R. 'Implementing Inner City Policy: Reflections from Experience', *Policy and Politics*, vol. 9 (1981).

Hampton, W. *Democracy and Community – a Study of Politics in Sheffield* (London: Oxford University Press, 1970).

Hashagan, S. 'Making and Breaking the Rules', *Strathclyde Studies in Community Work*, Occasional Papers, vol II (1982).

Henderson, P., Jones, D. and Thomas, D.N. *The Boundaries of Change in Community Work* (London: George Allen and Unwin, 1980).

Henderson, P. and Thomas, D.N. *Skills in Neighbourhood Work* (London: George Allen and Unwin, 1980).

Holterman, S. *Census Indicators of Urban Deprivation*, Working Note 6 (London: Department of the Environment, 1975).

Jacobs, S. *The Right to a Decent House* (London: Routledge and Kegan Paul, 1976).

Kramer, R.M. and Specht, H. (eds). *Readings in Community Organisation Practice* (Englewood Cliffs, New Jersey: Prentice Hall, 1969).

Lambert, J. 'Political Values and Community Work Practice' in Curno, P. (ed.) *Political Issues and Community Work* (London: Routledge and Kegan Paul, 1978).

Levin, P. 'Opening up the Planning Process' in Hatch, S. 'Towards Participation in Social Services', *Fabian Tract*, no. 419

(1973) reprinted in Henderson, P. and Thomas, D.N. *Readings in Community Work* (London: George Allen and Unwin, 1981).

Loney, M. *Community Against Government* (London: Heinemann Educational Books, 1983).

McConnell, C. *The Community Worker as Politicisor of the Deprived* (Edinburgh: Community Education Council, 1977).

—————. *Deprivation and Community Development Policy in Strathclyde – an Analysis and a Critique* (Dundee College of Education, 1978).

—————. 'Community Education in Scotland' in Smith, L. and Jones, D. *Deprivation, Participation and Community Action* (London: Routledge and Kegan Paul, 1981).

Mackay, S. and Herman, L. *A View from the Hill* (Paisley: Local Government Research Unit, Paisley College of Technology, 1980).

Marcuse, H. *One Dimensional Man* (Harmondsworth: Penguin, 1964).

Marris, P. *Meaning and Action: Community Planning and Conceptions of Change* (London: Routledge and Kegan Paul, 1987).

O'Brien, D.J. *Neighbourhood Organisation and Interest Group Processes* (Princeton University Press, 1975).

Payne, D. 'Job Satisfaction and Social Work' in Lishman J., *Social Work Departments as Organisations*, Research Highlights No. 4. (University of Aberdeen, 1984).

Perlman, R. and Gurin, A. *Community Organisation and Social Planning* (New York: John Wiley and Son, 1972).

Rossetti, F. 'Politics and Participation: A Case Study' in Curno, P. (ed.). *Political Issues and Community Work* (London: Routledge and Kegan Paul, 1978).

Runciman, W.G. *Relative Deprivation and Social Justice* (London: Routledge and Kegan Paul, 1966).

Schon, D. *Beyond the Stable State* (Harmondsworth: Pelican, 1973).

Seebohm, *Local Authority and Allied Personal Social Services* ('the Seebohm Report') (London: HMSO, 1968).

Skeffington, A.M. *People and Planning* ('the Skeffington Report') (London: HMSO, 1969).

Smith, G. *Social Work and the Sociology of Organisations* (London: Routledge and Kegan Paul, 1970).

Specht, H. 'The Dilemmas of Community Work in the United Kingdom', *Policy and Politics*, vol 4, no. 1 (1975).

Spergel, I.A. *Community Problem Solving – the Delinquency Example* (University of Chicago Press, 1969).

Stevenson, O. *Specialisation in Social Service Teams* (London: George Allen and Unwin, 1981).

Stevenson, O. and Parsloe, P. *Social Service Teams: The Practitioner's View* (London: HMSO, 1978).

Stewart, J., Spencer, K., Webster, B. *Local Government: Approaches to Urban Deprivation*, Occasional Paper No. 1 (London: Home Office Urban Deprivation Unit, 1976).

Strathclyde Region Social Work Department. 'Review of Community Work' (unpublished, 1989).

Strathclyde Regional Council. *Areas of Need – the Next Step* (1976).

————. *Generating Change: Urban Regeneration: The Strathclyde Experience: Opportunities for Private Investment* (1987).

————. *Multiple Deprivation* (1976).

————. *Social Strategy for the Eighties* (1985).

Thomas, D.N. *The Making of Community Work* (London: George Allen and Unwin, 1983).

————. 'Community Work, Social Change and Social Planning' in Curno, P. (ed.). *Political Issues and Community Work* (London: Routledge and Kegan Paul, 1978).

Thomas, D.N. and Warburton, R.W. *Community Workers in Social Service Departments: a Case Study* (London: National Institute for Social Work, 1977).

Twelvetrees A. *Community Work* (London: Macmillan, 1982).

————. 'A Personal View of Current Issues in Community Work', *Community Development Journal*, vol. 14, no. 3 (October 1979).

Waddington, P. 'Looking Ahead – Community Work into the 1980s', *Community Development Journal*, vol. 14, no. 3 (October, 1979).

Wedge, P. and Essen, J. *Children in Adversity* (London: National Children's Bureau and Pan, 1982).

Wedge, P. and Prosser, H. *Born to Fail* (London: National Children's Bureau and Arrow, 1973).

Worthington, A. *Policy Review Group on Community Development Services* ('the Worthington Report') (Strathclyde Regional Council, 1978).

Young, R. 'Community Development – its Political and Administrative Challenge', *Social Work Today* (February 1977) reprinted in Henderson, P. and Thomas, D.N. *Readings in Community Work* (London: George Allen and Unwin, 1981).

Index